CHILDREN'S
PLANET EARTH
ENCYCLOPEDIA

Clare Hibbert & Honor Head

ARCTURUS

ARCTURUS

This edition published in 2019 by Arcturus Publishing Limited
26/27 Bickels Yard, 151–153 Bermondsey Street,
London SE1 3HA

ISBN: 978-1-78828-607-7
CH006259NT
Supplier 41, Date 0419, Print run 7737

Consultant: Claudia Martin
Authors: Clare Hibbert @ Hollow Pond and Honor Head
Editors: Joe Harris, Donna Gregory, and Caroline Curtis
Designer: Amy McSimpson @ Hollow Pond

Printed in Malaysia

In this book, one billion means one thousand million (1,000,000,000) and one trillion means one million million (1,000,000,000,000).

CHILDREN'S PLANET EARTH ENCYCLOPEDIA

CONTENTS

Introduction

The study of our awe-inspiring planet is called geography. It covers everything from the atmosphere and weather to the stunning features of Earth's surface. Thanks to its water, our planet can support life of many kinds, including us. Geographers are also interested in how humans change Earth—for the better and the worse.

These are part of the Rockies, a mountain range along western North America.

Looking at the Land

Seven large landmasses called continents rise from the oceans. Part of Earth's crust, they are made of rock. Geography helps us to understand how physical features, such as mountain ranges and lakes, form.

Climate and Weather

Earth is surrounded by a layer of gases called the atmosphere. It protects us from the Sun's ultraviolet (UV) rays, but also traps its warmth. Changes in the atmosphere affect our local weather. The usual weather for a place is called its climate. Places near the equator have a warm, tropical climate.

Awesome Oceans

Salty seawater covers more than 70 percent of our planet, making it look blue from space. The oceans are home to 230,000 known species. They also provide us with food, water, energy, and transport, and they influence our weather, too.

Bangladesh has a tropical monsoon climate. Monsoons bring heavy rains from June to October. By the end of this rainy season, almost a fifth of Bangladesh is flooded.

Wind on the surface of our oceans whips up powerful waves.

Movements of Earth's crust pushed up rocks to form the Rocky Mountains 80-55 million years ago (mya). Creeping bodies of ice called glaciers carved the Rockies into shape.

Settlements and Cities

Natural forces have shaped our planet ... but so have humans! We've cleared land for settlements, farms, and industry, choosing places with fresh water, food, resources, and other advantages. Cities often developed along trade routes, at river crossings or beside sheltered bays.

Essaouira, on Morocco's Atlantic coast, has been a trading port for at least 2,500 years.

Moraine Lake in Alberta, Canada, freezes each winter and thaws in spring. Meltwater from a glacier fills it over the summer, so the water is highest (and most turquoise) in July.

The Environment

Our actions can harm the planet. For example, burning coal and other fossil fuels releases gases that damage our atmosphere. It's important to look after the environment so that there is still a wonderful world for future generations to enjoy.

Offshore turbines turn the wind's energy into electrical power. Unlike fossil fuels, the wind won't run out and it won't damage the atmosphere, either.

DID YOU KNOW? Earth's seven continents, from largest to smallest, are Asia, Africa, North America, South America, Antarctica, Europe, and Australasia.

Our Planet

Earth is one of eight planets orbiting our nearest star, the Sun, and the largest of the four rocky planets. Its position in the solar system (the region of space around the Sun) puts it in the "Goldilocks zone," where conditions are "just right" for water and life.

Earth's Birth

When our Sun began to shine about 4.6 billion years ago (bya), its gravity pulled nearby particles of dust, rock, gases, and ice into its orbit. They clumped into ball shapes—the planets.

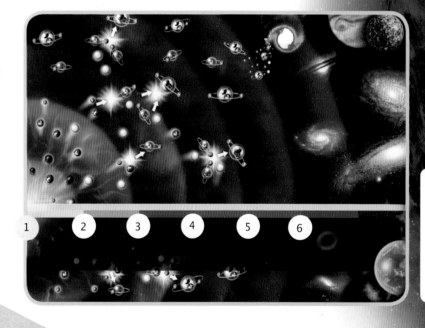

1. The Universe began 13.8 bya in a huge explosion called the Big Bang.

2. In the early Universe there was one force, the Super Force.

3. The Super Force split to create gravity, nuclear forces, and electromagnetism.

4. The Universe started to cool. Atomic nuclei could form.

5. After 300,000 years, the first atoms formed.

6. After one billion years, galaxies started to form.

PLANET EARTH FACTS

Average distance from the Sun: 149.6 million km (93 million miles)

Orbital speed: 108,000 km/h (67,000 mph)

Closest planet: Venus (at its closest it is 38 million km/ 24 million miles away, every 584 days)

Surface area: 510.1 million km^2 (196.9 million sq miles)

Earth

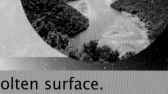

DID YOU KNOW? From 4.6 to 4 bya, Earth was hellishly hot, with a molten surface. This phase of its existence is called the Hadean Era after Hades, the Greek underworld.

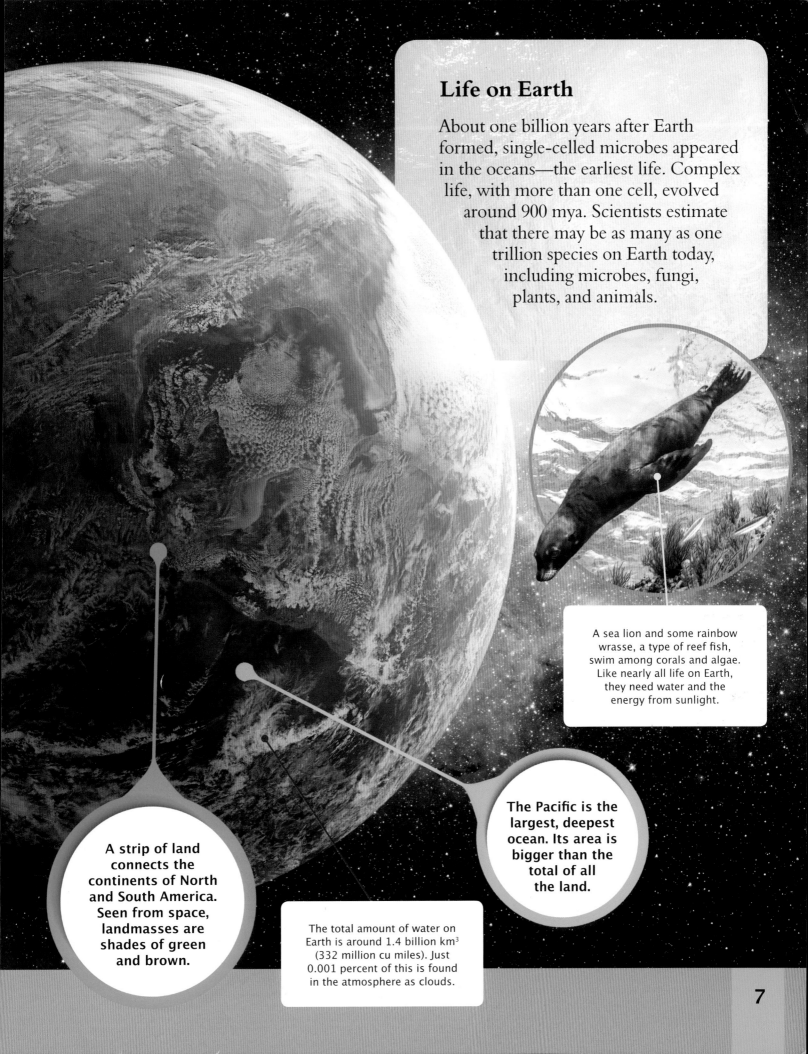

Life on Earth

About one billion years after Earth formed, single-celled microbes appeared in the oceans—the earliest life. Complex life, with more than one cell, evolved around 900 mya. Scientists estimate that there may be as many as one trillion species on Earth today, including microbes, fungi, plants, and animals.

A sea lion and some rainbow wrasse, a type of reef fish, swim among corals and algae. Like nearly all life on Earth, they need water and the energy from sunlight.

A strip of land connects the continents of North and South America. Seen from space, landmasses are shades of green and brown.

The Pacific is the largest, deepest ocean. Its area is bigger than the total of all the land.

The total amount of water on Earth is around 1.4 billion km³ (332 million cu miles). Just 0.001 percent of this is found in the atmosphere as clouds.

Seasons

It takes just over 365 days for Earth to travel around the Sun. During that time, which we call a year, we go through a cycle of seasons. There's a reason for the seasons! Earth is tilted on its axis (an imaginary line through its middle, from pole to pole). When places tilt toward the Sun, they receive more heat.

Four Seasons

Most places have four seasons—spring, summer, fall (autumn), and winter. When our hemisphere (half of the Earth) tilts toward the Sun, we have summer. When it tilts away, we have winter. June is summer in the north and winter in the south.

In fall (autumn) the leaves of deciduous trees lose their green pigment, chlorophyll. They turn shades of red, orange, and yellow.

Deciduous trees drop their leaves before winter. The leaves aren't tough enough to survive the winter cold.

MARCH

SUN

JUNE

SEPTEMBER

DECEMBER

In March, the northern hemisphere has spring, the season between winter and summer; the southern hemisphere has fall (autumn.)

In September, the southern hemisphere has spring; the northern hemisphere has fall (autumn), the season between summer and winter.

THREE SPRING EQUINOX FESTIVALS

Nowruz: Also called Persian New Year. People clean their houses, buy new clothes, and go on picnics.

Return of the Sun Serpent: At the Mayan temple in Chichen Itza, Mexico, sunlight and shadow create the illusion of a "snake" slithering down the steps.

Songkran: This Thai festival is traditionally held on April 13 every year. People celebrate with water fights!

Songkran

The fall (autumn) equinox is on 21, 22, 23, or 24 September in the northern half of the world and 19, 20, or 21 March in the south.

Two Seasons

In the area around the equator, called the tropics, the amount of sunlight and heat doesn't change much through the year. There are only two types of season—wet and dry. Temperatures are around 25°C (77°F) in the wet season and 20°C (68°F) in the dry.

In southern Asia, farmers plant rice at the start of the rainy season. Some still use water buffalo to prepare the fields.

DID YOU KNOW? Twice a year, in March and September, the Sun shines directly on the equator. These are called the equinoxes.

Day and Night

As well as orbiting the Sun, Earth spins on its axis (an imaginary line like a spinning top's spindle). It rotates once roughly every 24 hours. At any moment, half of our planet is facing toward the Sun (experiencing daytime) and half is facing away (experiencing night.)

Earth spins counterclockwise on its axis, giving us night and day.

Shortest and Longest

The northern hemisphere has most sunlight on June 21(its summer solstice) and least on December 21 (its winter solstice). It's the opposite in the southern hemisphere. The shortest day (winter solstice) is June 21 and the longest day (summer solstice) is December 21.

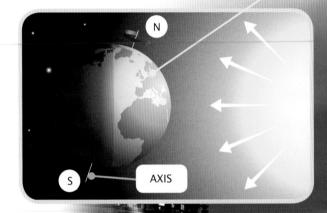

N

S

AXIS

What's the Time?

Before clocks, people told the time by the Sun. Midday was when the Sun is highest in the sky. Today we split the world into time zones. Each north-to-south strip has an agreed standard time.

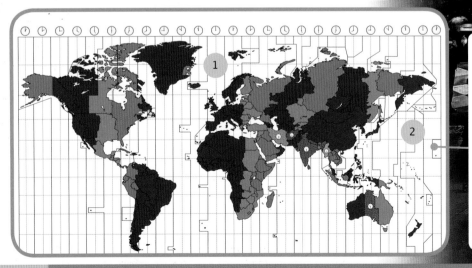

1

2

1. Standard time is measured in hours behind or ahead of this imaginary line, the Greenwich Meridian. The time here is called Greenwich Mean Time (GMT).

2. The International Date Line is halfway around the world from Greenwich. We gain a day if we cross it from west to east—Tuesday becomes Monday again.

DID YOU KNOW? One in every four years is a leap year with an extra day (February 29). Leap years keep our calendar in sync with our orbit around the Sun.

DAY AND NIGHT FACTS

Earth's rotational speed: 1,670 km/h (1,038 mph) at the equator.

Midnight sun: At the poles, the Sun never sets on the longest day—that's June for the north and December for the south.

Polar night: It's the opposite for the shortest day—that's June for the south and December for the north. At the poles, the Sun never rises.

Midnight sun in Norway

The night sky in the city is never really dark. There are too many artificial lights.

Except for where there are clouds, the daytime sky looks blue. This is because of the way the atmosphere scatters the light from the Sun.

Wherever we are in the world, the Sun always appears to "rise" in the east and set in the west. In reality, it's Earth that's moving.

This image is two photographs merged together to show Trafalgar Square, London, UK, at night and during the day.

Inside the Earth

Our planet is 12,742 km (7,918 miles) across and made up of layers, like an onion. The thin, outer layer of rocky land and seabed is the skin, or crust. It floats on a layer of semi-molten and solid rock called the mantle. Below that is Earth's superhot core.

Mostly Mantle

The mantle makes up about 84 percent of Earth's volume. Nearest the crust its rocks are 500–900°C (930–1,650°F). The temperature of the mantle rises by about 25°C per 1 km of depth (72°F per mile)—and the pressure also increases.

Volcanoes happen where molten rock from the mantle escapes through a hole in Earth's crust.

Down Under

Scientists have worked out Earth's mass from the effects of gravity at its surface, and discovered that Earth's core is super-dense. Iron is a heavy and common element, but there's not much of it in the crust. Earth's iron must have sunk to form most of its incredibly dense core.

A seismogram records the shockwaves from an earthquake. These waves can travel through solid materials, but not liquid. Studying seismograms showed scientists that at least part of Earth's core was liquid, not solid.

EARTH'S DEPTHS

Inner core: 1,220 km (760 miles) across

Outer core: 2,400 km (1,500 miles) thick

Mantle: 2,900 km (1,800 miles) thick

Crust: 5–50 km (3–30 miles) thick

Deepest artificial hole: 12.3 km (7.6 miles)

This tower stands over Russia's Kola Superdeep Borehole, a 12.3-km (7.6-mile) hole drilled into Earth's crust.

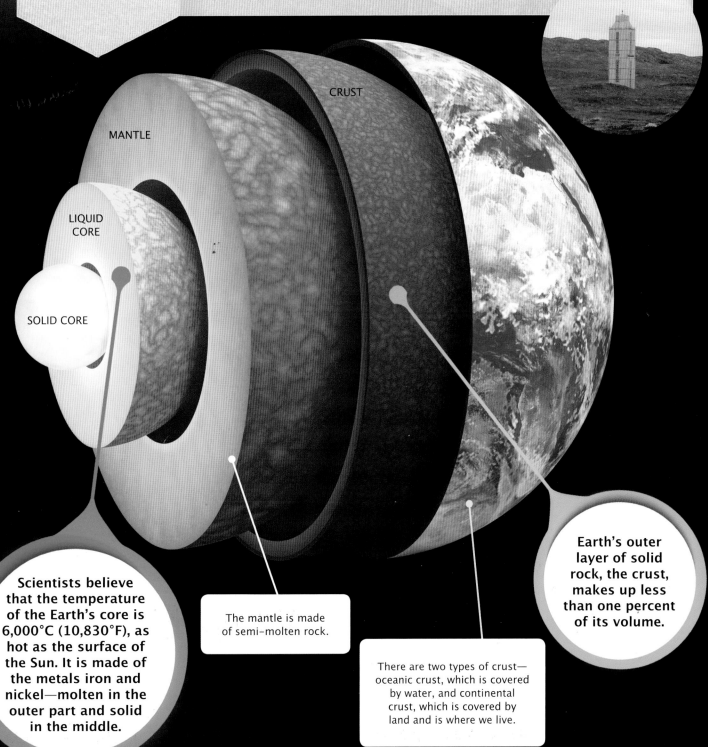

MANTLE

LIQUID CORE

SOLID CORE

CRUST

Scientists believe that the temperature of the Earth's core is 6,000°C (10,830°F), as hot as the surface of the Sun. It is made of the metals iron and nickel—molten in the outer part and solid in the middle.

The mantle is made of semi-molten rock.

There are two types of crust—oceanic crust, which is covered by water, and continental crust, which is covered by land and is where we live.

Earth's outer layer of solid rock, the crust, makes up less than one percent of its volume.

DID YOU KNOW? Earth's mass is 5,972 sextillion tonnes. That's 5,972 followed by 18 zeros (6,583 sextillion tons).

Magnetic Earth

Electromagnetism is one of the basic forces that affect how everything in the Universe behaves. Our planet is surrounded by its own electromagnetic field, the magnetosphere. Like a giant magnetic bubble, this force field shields our planet, keeping out radiation from our solar system and beyond.

Shape Shifter

The magnetosphere extends about 65,000 km (40,400 miles) into space on its Sun-facing side, which is flattened. Its other side trails around 600,000 km (370,000 miles) into space, like a comet's tail.

Circling liquid iron inside Earth's outer core generates electric currents. These produce the magnetosphere.

The Poles

Earth has magnetic north and south poles, close to the axis of its spin. They are not completely fixed, but they are the locations to which a compass points, north or south. Every few hundred thousand years, the magnetosphere flips and the direction of the poles reverses.

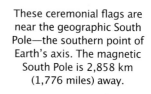

These ceremonial flags are near the geographic South Pole—the southern point of Earth's axis. The magnetic South Pole is 2,858 km (1,776 miles) away.

DID YOU KNOW? The magnetic South Pole moves about 10-15 km (6-9 miles) a year!

AURORA FACTS

1–5 days: Time it takes solar particles to reach Earth

11 years: Cycle of solar activity that affects aurorae

Seeing aurorae: Northern lights (best seen late August to April); southern lights (best seen March to September)

Other worlds: Venus, Mars, Jupiter, Saturn, Uranus, and Neptune all have aurorae

Solar flare

Earth's magnetic poles attract streams of space particles. Those that make it through the magnetosphere create a dazzling show of lights in the sky called an aurora.

When space particles crash into oxygen atoms, they make them glow green.

In the Arctic, the aurora is called the *aurora borealis* or northern lights. In Antarctica, it is the *aurora australis* or southern lights.

15

Shaping the Land

The "solid" rock beneath our feet is being reshaped all the time. A landslide, volcanic eruption, or meteorite impact can alter the landscape in a few seconds. Other processes, such as weathering and erosion, take hundreds of years.

Water, Ice, and Wind

If rainwater seeps into cracks in rocks and freezes, it expands, widens the gap, and shatters the rock. Rain and seawater can even dissolve some types of rock. Flowing rivers and creeping glaciers carve out deep canyons, and ocean waves break down cliffs. Strong winds carrying loose fragments can sculpt rocks, then dump fragments to form new land masses.

A glacier is a slow-moving "river" of ice. As it advances, it slices a steep-sided valley from the surrounding rock.

Making Islands

There are six main ways that islands can form:

CONTINENTAL ISLAND
Greenland is part of the same continental shelf as North America. A shallow, narrow sea separates them.

BARRIER ISLAND
Debris from ice-age glaciers created Germany's Sylt Island. Sand dumped by ocean waves has built it up.

ARTIFICIAL ISLAND
Palm Jumeirah, built off the coast of Dubai, is the world's largest artificial island. It's shaped like a palm tree!

TIDAL ISLAND
The land that connects Mont-Saint-Michel to mainland France is underwater at high tide.

OCEANIC ISLAND
Floreana is one of the Galápagos Islands. They formed from volcanoes that erupted on the ocean bed.

CORAL ISLAND
The Bahamas are formed from the hardened remains of tiny sea creatures called corals.

DID YOU KNOW? The Chicxulub impact threw up so much dust that it blocked out the Sun, changed the climate, and wiped out the non-avian dinosaurs.

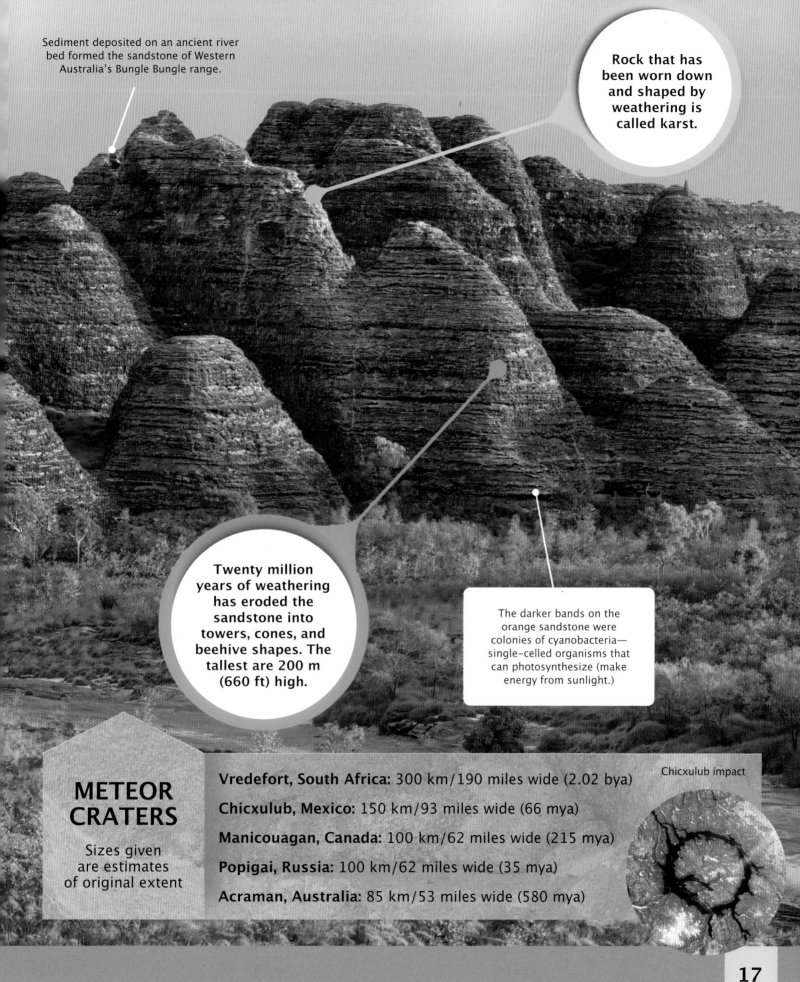

Sediment deposited on an ancient river bed formed the sandstone of Western Australia's Bungle Bungle range.

Rock that has been worn down and shaped by weathering is called karst.

Twenty million years of weathering has eroded the sandstone into towers, cones, and beehive shapes. The tallest are 200 m (660 ft) high.

The darker bands on the orange sandstone were colonies of cyanobacteria— single-celled organisms that can photosynthesize (make energy from sunlight.)

METEOR CRATERS

Sizes given are estimates of original extent

Vredefort, South Africa: 300 km/190 miles wide (2.02 bya)

Chicxulub, Mexico: 150 km/93 miles wide (66 mya)

Manicouagan, Canada: 100 km/62 miles wide (215 mya)

Popigai, Russia: 100 km/62 miles wide (35 mya)

Acraman, Australia: 85 km/53 miles wide (580 mya)

Chicxulub impact

Mountains

A mountain is land that is much taller than its surroundings, with sides that are steep or gently sloping. It can stand alone or be part of a chain, or range. Some of the world's most impressive mountain ranges are along boundaries between tectonic plates (see pages 26–7).

Folds and Fault-Blocks

Where two plates collide or one goes under another, rock can buckle. This pushes up fold mountains, which are rollercoaster-shaped. When the Indo-Australian and Eurasian plates began to collide about 50 mya, they created the Himalayan range in Asia. South America's Andes are fold mountains, too. If rock has a fault line (fracture), it breaks apart instead of folding. A block of rock is pushed up or tilted, creating a fault-block mountain, while the rock on either side stays as it is.

Stretching more than 7,000 km (4,300 miles), the Andes of South America are the longest mountain range on land, and one of the youngest.

The Sierra Nevada formed where the Pacific plate is moving under the North American one. These fault-block mountains have been pushed up and tilted.

The Andes formed about 45 mya, as the Nazca plate pushed under the South American plate, folding the rocks of the South American plate upward.

Guanacos live in the Andes. Their high concentration of red blood cells allows them to make the most of the limited oxygen.

Young and Old

Mountains with steep, jagged peaks are young—for mountains! Often, like the Himalayas and Andes, they are still growing. Older mountains have gentler, lower slopes that have been eroded over time (see page 16).

The Appalachians in eastern North America are one of the world's oldest mountain ranges. They formed around 480 mya— before the age of the dinosaurs.

HIGHEST MOUNTAINS
On each continent

Everest, Asia: 8,848 m (29,029 ft)
Aconcagua, S. America: 6,960 m (22,837 ft)
Denali, N. America: 6,190 m (20,310 ft)
Kilimanjaro, Africa: 5,895 m (19,341 ft)
Mount Elbrus, Europe: 5,642 m (18,510 ft)
Mount Vinson, Antarctica: 4,892 m (16,050 ft)
Puncak Jaya, Australasia: 4,884 m (16,024 ft)

Mount Kilimanjaro

DID YOU KNOW? As Mount Elbrus sits on the Europe–Asia boundary, some say Mont Blanc in the Alps is Europe's highest mountain, at 4,808 m (15,777 ft).

Earth's Atmosphere

Our planet is surrounded by a layer of gases called the atmosphere. Without it, life could not exist. The atmosphere provides us with oxygen to breathe and water to drink. It traps warmth from the Sun but it also shields us from dangerous rays.

Layers of Air

We divide the atmosphere into five layers, based on their temperature. We live and breathe in the troposphere. Its main gases are nitrogen (78 percent) and oxygen (21 percent).

At Esrange Space Center, Sweden, researchers launch stratospheric balloons into near-space. The launch site is the size of 40 soccer fields.

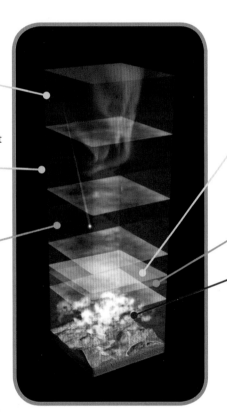

EXOSPHERE
Height: 500–10,000 km
 (310–6,200 miles)
Temperature: 0–1,700°C
 (32–3,092°F)
Features: Satellites and spacecraft

THERMOSPHERE
Height: 80–1,000 km
 (50–620 miles)
**Temperature increases with
 height:** 500–2,000°C
 (32–3,630°F)
Features: Aurorae

MESOSPHERE
Height: 50–80 km
 (31–50 miles)
**Temperature decreases with
 height:** –15°C to –101°C
 (5°F to –150°F)
Features: Meteor showers

STRATOSPHERE
Height: 10–50 km (6–31 miles)
Temperature increases with height:
 tropopause –50°C (–60°F);
 stratopause –15°C (5°F)
Features: Ozone layer, flight paths

OZONE LAYER
Height: 25 km (16 miles)

TROPOSPHERE
Height: up to 12 km (7.5 miles)
Temperature: surface 15°C (60°F);
 drops 6.5°C per 1,000 m
 (3.6°F per 1,000 ft)
Features: Weather

View of the atmosphere's layers

BETWEEN THE LAYERS

Exopause: Exosphere/outer space 10,000 km (6,200 miles)

Thermopause: Thermosphere/exosphere 1,000 km (620 miles)

Mesopause: Mesosphere/thermosphere 80 km (50 miles)

Stratopause: Stratosphere/mesosphere 50 km (31 miles)

Tropopause: Troposphere/stratosphere 12 km (7.5 miles)

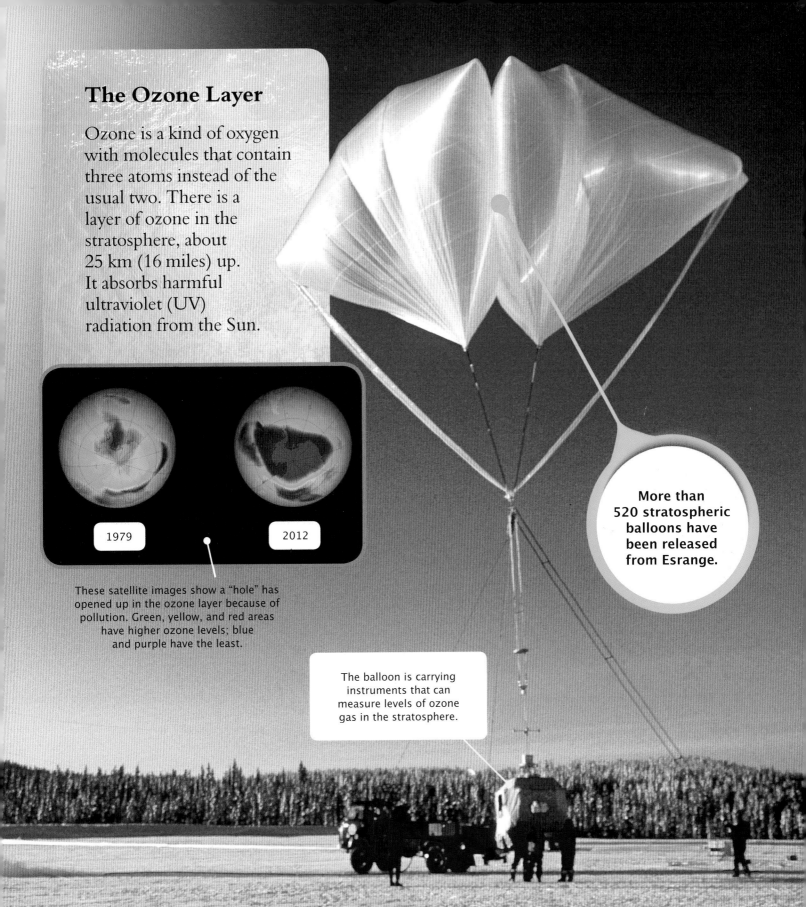

The Ozone Layer

Ozone is a kind of oxygen with molecules that contain three atoms instead of the usual two. There is a layer of ozone in the stratosphere, about 25 km (16 miles) up. It absorbs harmful ultraviolet (UV) radiation from the Sun.

1979

2012

These satellite images show a "hole" has opened up in the ozone layer because of pollution. Green, yellow, and red areas have higher ozone levels; blue and purple have the least.

More than 520 stratospheric balloons have been released from Esrange.

The balloon is carrying instruments that can measure levels of ozone gas in the stratosphere.

DID YOU KNOW? In the ionosphere, which stretches from the mesosphere into the exosphere, atoms are ionized (electrically charged) by solar rays.

Earth's Riches

From iron, oil, and silicon to animals, plants, fresh water, and wind ... resources are anything that people can use. Some exist naturally. Others are made by people from other resources—paper from trees, leather from animals, or plastics from oil.

Renewable or Non-Renewable

Oxygen, water, sunlight, and wind energy are all renewable. They won't run out during Earth's lifetime. Paper and leather are renewable too, because we can grow more trees and raise more animals. Non-renewables cannot be replaced—or they can, but it would take a very long time! Coal, oil, and natural gas take hundreds of millions of years to form from plant and animal remains.

Softwood, from firs, pines, and other conifers, is more renewable than hardwood. We can harvest it after about 40 years. Hardwood, from oak, beech, ash, and other broadleaved trees, takes centuries to mature.

RESOURCES RUNNING OUT ...

Coal: Reserves will run out by 2130

Natural gas: Reserves will run out by 2070

Oil: Reserves will run out by 2068

Helium: Won't run out, although it may become harder to obtain. It's released from radioactive elements as they decay, a process that takes billions of years.

Oil rig

DID YOU KNOW? Prehistoric people recycled! It was hard work mining metals from underground—so people melted and reused old gold, silver, or iron.

Hydroelectric power stations generate "clean" power from the energy of moving water. However, they also destroy habitats and sometimes force people from their homes.

Plastics

Plastics are made from non-renewable natural resources—oil, natural gas, and coal. Many are recyclable, but of the 272 million tonnes (300 million tons) of plastic produced each year, just 10 percent is recycled, and the rest piles up in landfill. Some companies are switching to packaging made from "biodegradable plastic," a plant-based material that *does* decompose.

Lake Gordon in Tasmania, southern Australia, was artificially formed by damming the Gordon River.

Every year about 8 million tonnes (8.8 million tons) of plastic are dumped in our oceans. Campaigners are fighting to reduce plastic waste.

A curved, 140 m/460 ft-high concrete wall blocks the flow of water and forces it down a shaft to turn turbines underground.

The power station beneath the reservoir can generate 432 megawatts (579,000 hp) of electricity.

Life on Earth

So far as we know, our planet is the only one in the solar system that has life. Every living and extinct species on Earth descended from the same living things, microbes that lived in the oceans around 3.6 bya.

What is Life?

Whether they're microbes, fungi, plants, or animals, all living organisms share certain characteristics. They are made up of one or more cells; they can reproduce, grow, and develop; they can obtain and use energy; and they can respond to their environment.

A single-celled amoeba reproduces by simply splitting itself in two. It's more complex for multi-celled life forms. It took two parents to produce these baby ring-tailed lemurs, which will need looking after for up to two years.

Surviving on Sunlight

Nearly all living things depend on the Sun. Plants, algae, and many bacteria, including those first microbes, photosynthesize (make energy directly from sunlight). Plant-eaters take in that energy indirectly when they consume plant foods. It then passes to the meat-eaters that consume the plant-eaters.

This photo is highly magnified. A harlequin poison frog is only about 3 cm (1.2 in) long!

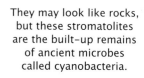

They may look like rocks, but these stromatolites are the built-up remains of ancient microbes called cyanobacteria.

Tropical rain forests are home to more than half the world's plants and animals. This harlequin poison frog lives on the forest floor in Colombia, South America.

Like many plants and animals, this frog has evolved protective features. Yellow–and–black markings warn predators that it is poisonous.

THE BIG FIVE MASS EXTINCTIONS

—and the proportion of species that died out in them

Ordovician–Silurian 444 mya: 85 percent of marine species

Late Devonian 407-359 mya: 75 percent of animal species

Permian–Triassic 266-252 mya: 95 percent of marine species (including all trilobites); 70 percent of land species

Triassic–Jurassic 201 mya: At least 50 percent of all species

Cretaceous 66 mya: 75 percent of animal species; many plants

Trilobite fossils

DID YOU KNOW? Plants began to grow on land from around 465 mya and land animals evolved about 397 mya.

Tectonic Plates

Earth's crust is broken up into seven large plates and about a dozen smaller ones. They drift on the mantle, the layer of semi-molten rock beneath them. Over Earth's history, their constant movement has formed and pulled apart continents, created volcanoes, and shaped mountains (see pages 18–19).

Giant Jigsaw

Today's major tectonic plates fit together like a jigsaw. They have three types of boundary—convergent (moving together), divergent (moving apart), or transform (sliding past each other). Earthquakes and volcanoes are most common along plate boundaries.

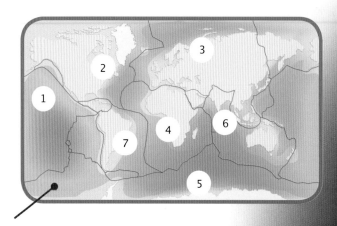

MAJOR TECTONIC PLATES

1. Pacific Plate
2. North American Plate
3. Eurasian Plate
4. African Plate
5. Antarctic Plate
6. Indo–Australian Plate
   (broken into Australian and Indian plates)
7. South American Plate

Plate Boundaries

CONVERGENT

The Eurasian and Australian plates have a convergent boundary that has pushed up this volcano complex in East Java, Indonesia.

DIVERGENT

The Eurasian and North American plates have a divergent boundary. As they pull apart, they are opening up this rift in Iceland.

TRANSFORM

California's San Andreas fault is along a transform boundary. The North American and Pacific plates are sliding past each other.

DID YOU KNOW? Tectonic plates move 3-5 cm (1-2 in) a year.

THE SEVEN MAJOR PLATES

—and their size

Pacific: 103.3 million sq km (40 million sq miles)
North American: 75.9 million sq km (29.3 million sq miles)
Eurasian: 67.8 million sq km (26.2 million sq miles)
African: 61.3 million sq km (23.7 million sq miles)
Antarctic: 60.9 million sq km (23.5 million sq miles)
Indo–Australian: 58.9 million sq km (22.7 million sq miles)
South American: 43.6 million sq km (16.8 million sq miles)

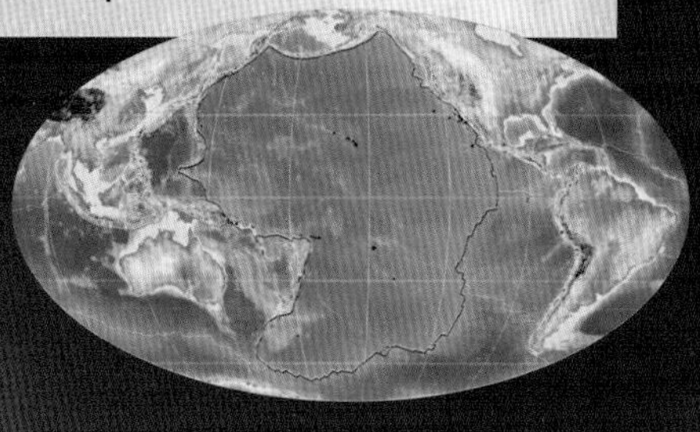

Pacific Plate

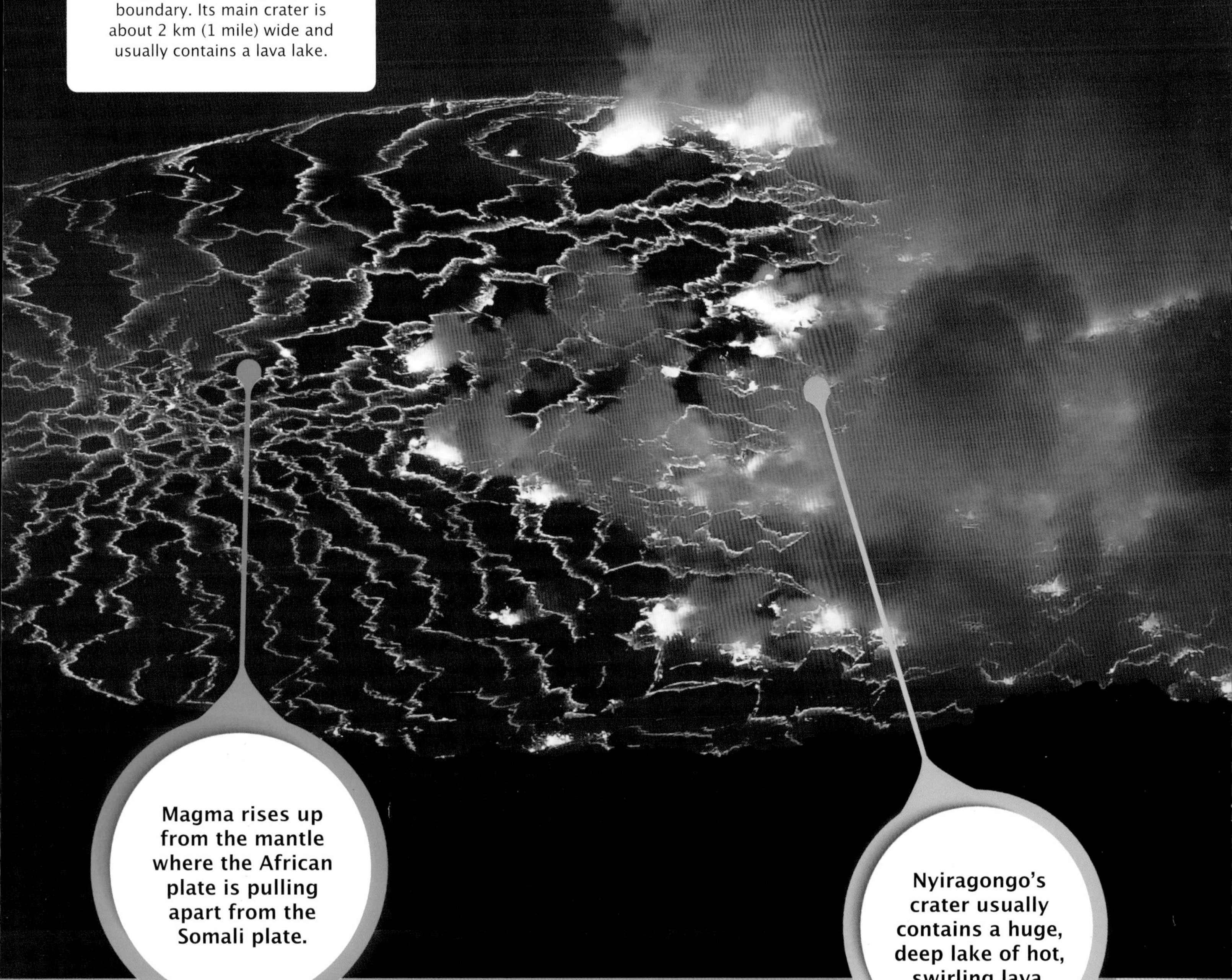

Mount Nyiragongo in the Democratic Republic of Congo is on a divergent plate boundary. Its main crater is about 2 km (1 mile) wide and usually contains a lava lake.

Magma rises up from the mantle where the African plate is pulling apart from the Somali plate.

Nyiragongo's crater usually contains a huge, deep lake of hot, swirling lava.

Volcanoes

A volcano is a place where magma (molten rock) pushes up through Earth's crust from the mantle below. Once it erupts at the surface, this molten rock is called lava. Over time, layers of lava and ash cool, harden, and build up.

Where in the World?

Volcanoes form at tectonic plate boundaries (see page 26). At a divergent boundary, where plates are moving apart, magma pushes up along the crack. At a convergent boundary, where plates are pushing together, folding rock can fracture and magma escapes. A few volcanoes form in the middle of plates, over "hot spots" on Earth's crust.

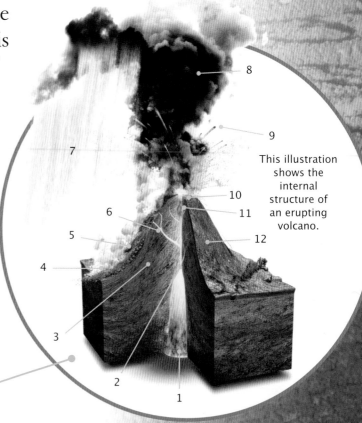

This illustration shows the internal structure of an erupting volcano.

PARTS OF A VOLCANO

1. Magma chamber
2. Pipe
3. Layers of hardened lava, ash, and rock from earlier eruptions
4. Pyroclastic flow (hot gas, ash, and rock)
5. Lava
6. Dyke (side vent)
7. Acid rain from ash cloud
8. Ash cloud
9. Lava bomb
10. Crater
11. Vent
12. Flanks (slopes)

Volcano Shapes

The shape of a volcano is decided by the way it erupts, and the type of lava that flows from it.

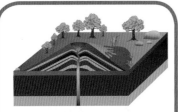

CINDER CONE
Blobs of thick lava shoot into the air, break into bits, and fall as cinders. They form a low cone around the vent.

STRATOVOLCANO
Thick, sticky lava explodes from the volcano, along with ash and rock. They form a steep, pointed cone.

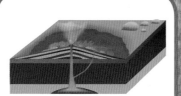

SHIELD VOLCANO
Thin, runny lava flows gently from the volcano. It spreads out and hardens into a low, flat mound.

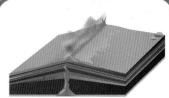

FISSURE VENT VOLCANO
Lava seeps (or, occasionally, explodes) from a long crack. It can harden into low "beds" of volcanic rock.

Any volcano that's erupting now, or has erupted in the last few centuries, is described as active.

There are 1,500 active volcanoes worldwide, and 127 of them are in Indonesia. Mount Slamet in Central Java, Indonesia, is an active stratovolcano.

Mount Slamet isn't erupting but steam is escaping through the vent. It also releases several gases, including carbon dioxide and chlorine.

Laki today

THE MOST TERRIBLE FISSURE IN HISTORY

1783–4: Iceland's Laki fissure erupted for eight months.

14 cubic km (3.4 cubic miles) of basalt lava were released.

20 villages were destroyed by lava flows.

75 percent of cattle and sheep were killed by eating poisoned grass.

9,000 Icelanders were killed in the resulting famine.

DID YOU KNOW? A volcano that's not active but may erupt again is described as dormant (sleeping). One that will never erupt again is called extinct.

Eruption!

As well as lava, eruptions throw out ash, dust, and rock. Lava bombs are blobs of lava that harden in mid–air. They range from 6.4 cm (2.5 in) across to 6 m (20 ft).

Up to 10 volcanoes are erupting around the world at this moment. Before an eruption, hot, molten magma pushes up from the mantle and collects in a chamber under the volcano. The pressure builds … until the volcano erupts.

Energy Release

An eruption can be a sudden, huge explosion or a slower, gentle flow. It can go on for hours, days, weeks, or years. Its power is measured using the Volcanic Explosivity Index (VEI), a scale that goes from 0 to 8. Each step up the scale is ten times stronger than the last.

Types of Eruption

Types of eruption are usually named after the place they were first observed, but Plinian eruptions are named after the Roman writer Pliny. He described the eruption of Mount Vesuvius that destroyed the towns of Pompeii and Herculaneum in 79 CE.

STROMBOLIAN
Small, regular gas explosions —and occasional stronger ones—throw out arcs of sticky, glowing lava.

HAWAIIAN
This is the gentlest kind of eruption. Fluid, basalt–type lava runs down the sides of the volcano.

PLINIAN
A huge explosion launches a plume of lava, ash, and rock that then thunders down the slopes as pyroclastic flow.

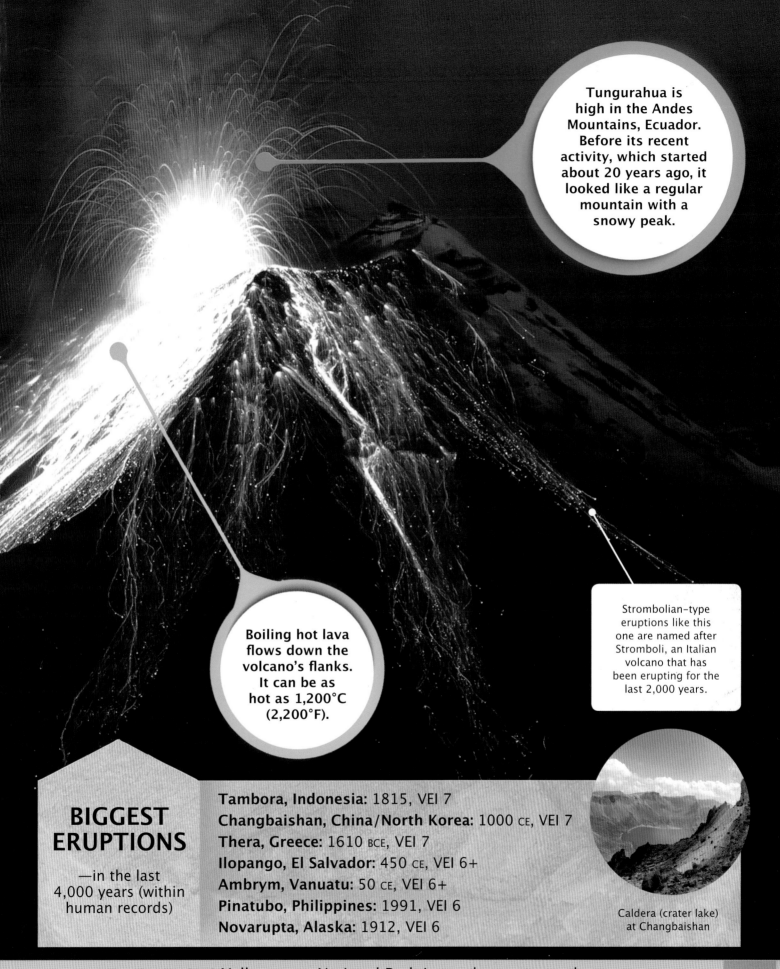

Tungurahua is high in the Andes Mountains, Ecuador. Before its recent activity, which started about 20 years ago, it looked like a regular mountain with a snowy peak.

Strombolian-type eruptions like this one are named after Stromboli, an Italian volcano that has been erupting for the last 2,000 years.

Boiling hot lava flows down the volcano's flanks. It can be as hot as 1,200°C (2,200°F).

BIGGEST ERUPTIONS
—in the last 4,000 years (within human records)

Tambora, Indonesia: 1815, VEI 7
Changbaishan, China/North Korea: 1000 CE, VEI 7
Thera, Greece: 1610 BCE, VEI 7
Ilopango, El Salvador: 450 CE, VEI 6+
Ambrym, Vanuatu: 50 CE, VEI 6+
Pinatubo, Philippines: 1991, VEI 6
Novarupta, Alaska: 1912, VEI 6

Caldera (crater lake) at Changbaishan

DID YOU KNOW? Yellowstone National Park is one huge supervolcano. It's had three VEI-8 eruptions—2.1 mya, 1.3 mya, and 640,000 years ago.

Rivers of Fire

Magma is molten rock. The way in which it erupts as lava depends on the kind of rock and its silica content (silica is the mineral that forms sand).

Temperature

Lava without much silica is usually runny. The most common lava of this type is basalt. Lava that contains lots of silica is very viscous (sticky). An example is rhyolitic lava, which forms from granite-type rocks. Andesitic lava is halfway between the two. Lava's viscosity and temperature affect how fast it flows.

Pahoehoe (say "pah-hoy-hoy") is basaltic lava. After its top layer forms a skin, it still flows underneath, pulling the surface into twisted, rope-like folds.

Basalt forms from the rapid cooling of magma near the surface of the Earth. If magma is trapped beneath the surface, it will cool more slowly and form gabbro.

Mount Etna in Italy produces basaltic lava. This type of lava is high in iron and magnesium and low in silica.

LAVA TYPES	Viscosity	Silica content	Eruption temperature
Basaltic	Low	45–55%	1,000–1,200°C (1,832–2,192°F)
Andesitic	Medium	55–65%	800–1,000°C (1,472–1,832°F)
Rhyolitic	High	65–75%	650–800°C (1,202–1,472°F)

Ollagüe, Chile-Bolivia, an andesite volcano

Rivers of Mud

If the volcano has a cap of snow and ice, or if it erupts during heavy rains, lots of water mixes with the lava or pyroclastic flow. The result is deadly mudflows called lahars. Torrents of mud gush down the sides of the volcano at speeds of up to 80 km/h (50 mph).

This village was engulfed by a lahar after Indonesia's Mount Merapi erupted during the rainy season.

Hot, runny lava has fewer gas bubbles. It's not as explosive as stickier lavas.

DID YOU KNOW? When Nevado del Ruiz erupted in 1985, lahars destroyed the town of Armero in Colombia, killing 20,000 of the 29,000 inhabitants.

33

Living with Volcanoes

Small craters dot the rim of Lake Batur in Bali, Indonesia. The lake is a caldera that formed more than 20,000 years ago inside one of the volcano Mount Batur's previous craters.

Volcanoes cause deaths and terrible destruction, so why do people carry on living near them? Useful rocks and minerals form inside volcanoes, including precious gems. Eruptions produce ash that fertilizes the soil.

Volcanic Treasures

Basalt, pumice, ash, and perlite all come from volcanoes and are used in building materials, including concrete, cement, insulation, and plaster. Pumice is an ingredient in many cleaning products, too. Poisonous sulfur from volcanoes is an incredibly useful mineral, used to bleach sugar, make matches and fertilizer, and vulcanize (harden) rubber.

Four farming villages are based on the slopes of Mount Batur. The fertile soil yields healthy crops of peppers, tomatoes, onions, and other crops.

Indonesia is the last place on Earth where sulfur is extracted by hand. The miners risk their lives every day.

Mount Batur is still active, and almost half a million people live within 5 km (3 miles) of it.

Volcano Scientists

Volcanologists record eruptions and study samples of lava, rock, mud, and gas. Their hi-tech instruments detect tiny changes in volcanic activity. They can predict an eruption in time to move people to safety.

Balinese people use mineral-rich water from Lake Batur on their crops. They also farm fish in the lake.

This volcanologist is downloading data from a research sensor. She is checking on Mount Erebus, an active volcano on Ross Island, Antarctica.

VOLCANIC FIELDS CLOSE TO PEOPLE

Population within 5 km (3 miles)

Michoacán-Guanajuato, Mexico: (5.8 million)

Tatun, Taiwan: (5 million)

Campi Flegrei, Italy: (2.2 million)

Ilopango, El Salvador: (2 million)

Hainan Volcanic Field, China: (1.7 million)

Parícutin had a VEI-4 eruption in 1943—the most recent in the Michoacán–Guanajuato field.

DID YOU KNOW? Campi Flegrei is an area of volcanic activity west of Naples, Italy. Experts believe it could produce a VEI-7 eruption.

Volcanic Islands

Volcanoes create as well as destroy, building up new land from the sea. Tens of millions of years ago they pushed up the Canary Islands in the Atlantic; the Galápagos formed five to three million years ago; and the Indonesian islands of Bali and Java emerged in the last two to three million years.

Building Up

There are more than a million submarine volcanoes around the world—places on the sea floor where magma can erupt. Most are along plate boundaries (see page 26), but about a quarter are on hot spots. If cooled lava builds up high enough, a new island rises from the ocean.

Sakurajima is a volcanic island in southern Japan which formed about 13,000 years ago. It is home to around 5,000 people.

Five volcanoes over a hot spot formed the island of Hawaii. Kilauea is the most active. As its lava cools in the sea, the island grows.

NEWEST VOLCANIC ISLANDS

Nishinoshima, Japan: Formed its current size 2013–16.

Hunga Tonga–Hunga Ha'apai, Tonga: Formed its current size 2009.

Surtsey, Iceland: Formed 1963–7.

Anak Krakatoa, Indonesia: Formed 1927–30.

Kavachi, Solomon Islands: Formed at least nine times since 1939.

Anak Krakatoa

DID YOU KNOW? All eight main Hawaiian islands are volcanoes. Kauai appeared first, around 5.1 mya. Hawaii itself is just 300,000 years old.

The Story of Surtsey

Witnessed by the crew of a fishing boat, the island of Surtsey rose out of the ocean southwest of Iceland on 14 November 1963. It was created by a series of explosive volcanic eruptions on a plate boundary called the Mid-Atlantic Ridge.

Sakurajima erupts almost every day. It's one of Japan's most active volcanoes.

Surtsey, seen here from the air, is named after Surtr, a fire giant in Norse mythology.

Sakurajima's fertile slopes are famous for their enormous daikon radishes and tiny mandarin oranges.

More than 600,000 people live in Kagoshima, 8 km (5 miles) across the bay from Sakurajima. The city is regularly showered with ash.

Earthquakes

Like volcanoes, earthquakes cause terrible destruction. Their powerful shock waves spread out from a central point, shaking the ground and collapsing houses and roads. Earthquakes also trigger follow-on disasters.

Horrible Hazards

Earthquakes in mountainous areas set off landslides, mudslides, and avalanches. If they happen under the sea, they create tsunamis (see pages 42–3)—enormous tidal waves that surge onto the land. Floods also happen when earthquakes break dams or flood barriers. Fires start if power stations crumble or gas pipes burst.

Aftershocks may follow the initial destruction, and there may be damage as the ground settles. Falling masonry (bricks, stones, and tiles) can hit or bury people.

Rescue workers use sniffer dogs and infrared detectors to locate people who are trapped in the rubble.

Nepal lies on the boundary where the Indian Plate is pushing under the Eurasian Plate.

How Earthquakes Happen

Earthquakes occur at tectonic plate boundaries. If the moving plates "snag" on each other, pressure builds along fractures called faults. When the plates break free, the sudden jolt causes an earthquake.

NORMAL FAULT

Rock on one side of the fault drops down compared to the rock on the other side.

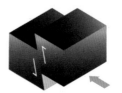

REVERSE FAULT

Rock on one side of the fault is pushed up compared to the rock on the other side.

SLIP FAULT

Rock on either side of the fault moves horizontally in opposite directions.

The earthquake that struck Nepal in 2015 was magnitude 7.8.

EARTHQUAKE MAGNITUDE SCALE
The strength, or magnitude, of an earthquake is measured by a number from 1 to 10.

MICRO
1.0–1.9

MINOR
2.0–3.9

LIGHT
4.0–4.9

MODERATE
5.0–5.9

STRONG
6.0–6.9

MAJOR
7.0–7.9

GREAT
8.0 or more

The April 2015 Nepal earthquake killed nearly 9,000 people, injured more than 23,000, and left nearly 3.5 million people homeless.

WORST QUAKE FATALITIES

825,000: Shaanxi, China, 23 January 1556 (8.0)

255,000: Tangshan, China, 28 July 1976 (7.8)

250,000: Antioch, Turkey, 21 May 526 (7.0)

235,000: Haiyuan, China, 16 December 1920 (7.8)

230,000: Aleppo, Syria, 11 October 1138 (magnitude 8.5)

Tangshan earthquake, 1976

DID YOU KNOW? American seismologist Charles Richter created an accurate earthquake magnitude scale in 1935.

Earthquake Plans

Experts can locate plate boundaries and faults, so they know *where* earthquakes are likely to occur—but can they tell *when*? Seismologists (people who study earthquakes) do their best to give early warnings. In the meantime, people who live in the danger zones stay prepared.

Planning Ahead

In earthquake drills, people learn how to react quickly and safely. "Safe spots" are identified in rooms that are often used. Instruction includes where to find a first aid kit, and how to turn off water, gas, and electricity supplies.

This is a drill. When the earthquake alarm sounds, the children adopt a safe position to protect their head from falling debris.

This research station is at Parkfield, on California's San Andreas Fault.

Building for Stability

When the ground shakes strongly, it can behave like water. This is called liquefaction. Without support, buildings sink into the ground. Architects earthquake-proof their designs by constructing on flexible foundations. The skyscrapers sway, but they don't fall down.

Japan has had earthquake-proof buildings for more than 1,400 years. The stories of a pagoda fit loosely around a central, cedar pole that wobbles with the seismic waves.

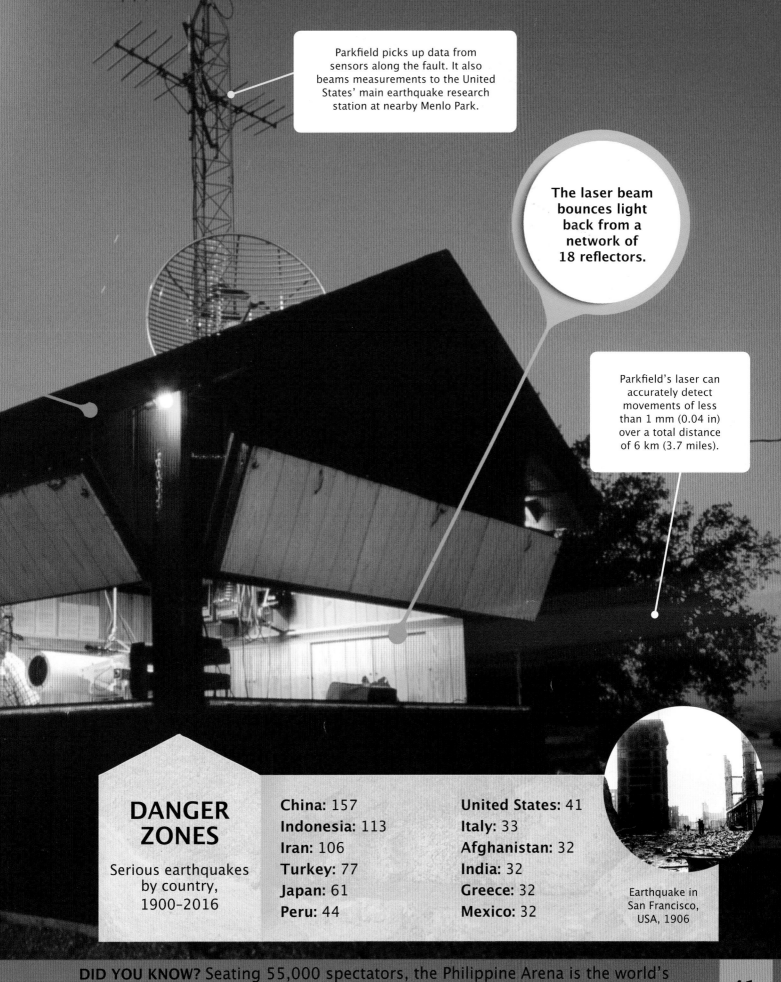

Parkfield picks up data from sensors along the fault. It also beams measurements to the United States' main earthquake research station at nearby Menlo Park.

The laser beam bounces light back from a network of 18 reflectors.

Parkfield's laser can accurately detect movements of less than 1 mm (0.04 in) over a total distance of 6 km (3.7 miles).

DANGER ZONES

Serious earthquakes by country, 1900–2016

China: 157	United States: 41
Indonesia: 113	Italy: 33
Iran: 106	Afghanistan: 32
Turkey: 77	India: 32
Japan: 61	Greece: 32
Peru: 44	Mexico: 32

Earthquake in San Francisco, USA, 1906

DID YOU KNOW? Seating 55,000 spectators, the Philippine Arena is the world's largest indoor arena—and it's built to survive a magnitude 8 earthquake.

Tsunamis

Although they're sometimes called tidal waves, tsunamis have nothing to do with the tides. These gigantic walls of water are usually set off by an underwater earthquake. Volcanic eruptions, underwater explosions, and meteorite impacts can also cause them.

Journey to Shore

When a section of seabed suddenly rises or falls, it shifts a huge amount of water outward. The tsunami picks up height as it enters shallower waters and hits the shore as a series of waves. Sometimes the tsunami sucks up all the coastal waters a few minutes before it strikes, adding to its total volume.

This devastation was caused by the 2004 Indian Ocean earthquake and tsunami.

Japanese artist Hokusai produced this woodblock print, *The Great Wave*, around 1830. It shows a tsunami about to engulf what is now Yokohama.

THE WORST TSUNAMI IN HISTORY
26 December 2004

230,000 people killed in 14 different countries

1.74 million people left homeless

9.1–9.3: Magnitude of the earthquake

800 km/h (500 mph): Speed of the tsunami

3 waves hit Sumatra (the second was the strongest)

Survivors in a shelter camp

DID YOU KNOW? When the Portuguese capital, Lisbon, was hit by a tsunami on 1 November 1755, around 1 in 5 people in the area lost their lives.

An earthquake off the coast of Sumatra, Indonesia, triggered the tsunami. The waves were up to 30 m (100 ft) high.

Leupung, on Sumatra's west coast, was one of the closest towns to the earthquake's central point. Out of a population of 10,000, just 500 survived.

Indonesia was the country hardest hit by the tsunami, with nearly 170,000 dead and more than 500,000 homeless.

Tsunami Trackers

Eighty percent of tsunamis happen around the edge of the Pacific Ocean. Twenty-six nations around the Pacific rely on the Pacific Tsunami Warning System, based in Hawaii. It monitors water levels and seismic (earthquake) activity.

This computer model shows the tsunami that hit northeastern Japan in March 2011. Wave heights are coded from yellow (shallow) to black (high).

43

Springs and Geysers

Hot springs and spurting geysers are "geothermal" (heated by the Earth.) They happen when magma or hot rocks heat groundwater. Geothermal features occur near volcanoes.

Health-Giving Spas

Many people like to bathe in hot springs. It relaxes the mind and body, and soothes aches and pains. The water also contains minerals such as silica and sulfur, which can treat skin conditions.

Iceland's popular Blue Lagoon isn't a natural hot spring, but its waters *are* geothermally heated. It's fed by the nearby geothermal power station, which collects hot water from 2,000 m (6,560 ft) underground.

THREE AMAZING SPRINGS

Pamukkale, Turkey: Hot springs on white terraces of travertine, a limestone formed from deposits of minerals in the water.

Steamboat Springs, USA: Bubbling hot springs in Colorado which sound like a chugging steamboat.

Waiotapu, New Zealand: Hot springs in shades of yellow, green, turquoise, and orange.

One of the hot springs at Waiotapu, New Zealand

DID YOU KNOW? The hot springs and geysers at Yellowstone National Park, USA, produce around 300 million watts of heat energy.

Geothermal Features

Hot springs are pools of hot water. Geysers are springs that spurt sprays of hot air and water into the air. Fumaroles are cracks in the ground that shoot out hot steam and gas. Mudpots are pools of hot, bubbling mud.

The water in an onsen (Japanese for "hot spring") can reach very high temperatures.

HVERAROND, ICELAND
Close to Namafjall volcano, this fumarole is giving off sulfurous steam and other gases.

STROKKUR GEYSER, ICELAND
This geyser shoots a boiling fountain of hot water into the air every six to ten minutes.

WAIOTAPU, NEW ZEALAND
Like most geothermal features, mudpots smell of rotten eggs. They contain mud or clay.

Japanese macaques are nicknamed "snow monkeys." They live further north than any other primate, except humans.

Japan has more than 3,000 hot springs.

Geological Time

It's mind-boggling to imagine Earth's 4.6-million-year lifespan. Geologists (scientists who study rocks) break it down into smaller, more manageable chunks. The largest of these are eons which, in turn, are split into smaller divisions called eras.

From Eras to Epochs

The current Cenozoic Era began 66 million years ago (mya) with the extinction event that wiped out the dinosaurs at the end of the Mesozoic. Eras split into periods. The Mesozoic had three—the Triassic, Jurassic, and Cretaceous. Periods split into epochs. Our Holocene epoch began at the end of the last Ice Age, 11,000 years ago.

These towers in Wulingyuan, southeastern China, are made of rock that is more than 400 million years old.

EONS AND ERAS

Eon	Era	Dates (mya)
Phanerozoic	Cenozoic	66–0
	Mesozoic	252–66
	Paleozoic	541–252
Proterozoic	Neoproterozoic	1,000–541
	Mesoproterozoic	1,600–1,000
	Paleoproterozoic	2,500–1,600
Archean	Neoarchean	2,800–2,500
	Mesoarchean	3,200–2,800
	Paleoarchean	3,600–3,200
	Eoarchean	4,000–3,600
Hadean		4,600–4,000

If we picture geological time, we can see that humans have been around for only a fraction of it.

THE SPIRAL OF TIME

1. Earth forms 4.6 bya
2. Single-celled life 3.6 bya
3. Multicellular life 900 mya
4. Trilobite 510 mya
5. Life on land 440 mya
6. Age of Reptiles— the Mesozoic, 252–66 mya
7. Age of Mammals— the Cenozoic, from 66 mya
8. Modern humans evolve— around 200,000 years ago

DID YOU KNOW? Geological time intervals are decided using key events, such as extinctions. That's why they aren't equal in length like minutes in an hour.

Dating Rocks

Geologists work out the age of rocks by comparing layers from different places and matching the fossils, minerals, or rocks. Radiometric dating is a more complex method that uses radioactive materials.

Fossils in sedimentary rocks gave geologists the first clues that rocks contain a record of Earth's history.

These geologists are drilling a 1-m (3.3-ft) core sample of coral. A coral colony's layers store data about changing conditions in the oceans.

Sedimentary rock is one of the three types of rock—the others are igneous and metamorphic. Each forms in a different way.

Wulingyuan has more than 3,000 quartzite sandstone pillars.

Igneous Rocks

When hot, molten rock called magma cools, it solidifies into igneous rock. Some igneous rock forms above ground, from magma that erupted from a volcano as lava. "Plutonic" igneous rock forms below ground. It is named after Pluto, Greek god of the underworld.

Top Rocks

There are more than 900 types of igneous rock. The two most common families are basalt and granite, which come in different hues depending on the minerals they contain. Granite, named for its graininess, can be pink, red, brown, green, blue, or black.

Fingal's Cave is on Staffa, an island off the west coast of Scotland. It has three layers of igneous rock.

These "fairy chimneys" in central Turkey formed from tuff (cooled volcanic ash) and basalt. Some of the softer tuff has worn away over the millennia, creating magical shapes.

IGNEOUS MONUMENTS

Great Zimbabwe, Zimbabwe: Granite

Moai statues, Easter Island, Chile: Basalt

Monument to the Equator, Ecuador: Andesite

Mount Rushmore: Fine-grained granite

Temple-Pyramid, Copán, Honduras: Tuff

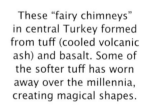

Mount Rushmore

DID YOU KNOW? Ninety percent of Earth's crust is igneous rock, but most of it is buried under layers of sedimentary rock.

The top layer of the cave is formed from glassy basalt.

Fingal's Cave and the Giant's Causeway in Northern Ireland formed at the same time. They both have columns of basalt that are mostly six-sided.

The middle layer of the cave has up to 40,000 pillars of fine-grained black basalt. They formed around 60 mya.

The bottom layer of the cave is tuff.

Common Igneous Rocks

PUMICE
This porous rock is light enough to float on water. It forms from frothy lavas such as rhyolite.

OBSIDIAN
This glassy rock forms when viscous lava with a high silica content cools so fast that no crystals can form.

MICROGABBRO
This fine-grained rock forms underground from basalt-type lava that poured into cracks in existing rock.

Sedimentary Rocks

When grains of rock, pebbles, mud, sand, and shells are pressed together over millions of years, they form layers of sedimentary rock. Other sedimentary rocks form from dissolved minerals left behind after water in a lake or sea dries up.

Super Strata

Sedimentary rock forms strata (layers) that date to different times—the oldest are at the bottom. If the strata aren't horizontal, the land has moved since the rock formed. Sedimentary rock sometimes contains animal or plant remains that fossilized in the sediment.

Monument Valley is on the Arizona-Utah border, USA. Its distinctive rock formations were created by weathering over millions of years.

The valley is dotted with flat-topped sandstone structures called buttes.

The sedimentary rock layers that make up China's Rainbow Mountains formed in the Cretaceous. They were pushed up by plate movement about 55 mya.

The siltstone on the valley floor has a blueish hue because it contains manganese oxide.

SEDIMENTARY MONUMENTS

Abu Simbel, Egypt: Sandstone

Angkor Wat, Cambodia: Sandstone

Uluru (Ayer's Rock), Australia: Sandstone

Empire State Building, USA: Limestone cladding

Colosseum, Italy: Travertine (a type of limestone)

Great Temple of Ramesses II, Abu Simbel, Egypt

Each butte has a top layer of red sandstone, a middle layer of paler Permian sandstone, and a base of shale.

Common Sedimentary Rocks

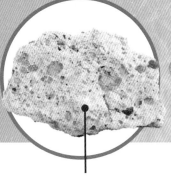

TUFA
Tufa forms when a body of water evaporates, leaving a crust of minerals. As in all limestones, the main minerals are calcite and aragonite from the skeletons of marine animals.

CONGLOMERATE
Larger chunks, known as clasts, are held together by a finer grained sediment— usually sand, silt, or clay. Conglomerate sometimes forms from debris dumped by glaciers.

CHALK
Chalk is made entirely of calcite from the shells of ancient, microscopic sea creatures. It is a soft rock, with very fine grains. It does not erode as much as other limestones.

DID YOU KNOW? Sedimentary rocks cover about three-quarters of Earth's surface but make up only five percent of its crust.

Metamorphic Rocks

A caterpillar transforms itself into a butterfly in a process called metamorphosis, meaning "changing form." Metamorphic rocks are any rocks that have been completely transformed by heat and pressure, or just heat, from deep within the Earth.

Degrees of Pressure

When shale, a sedimentary rock, comes under low pressure, it turns into fine-grained slate. Under medium pressure and heat, slate (and many other rocks) becomes medium-grained schist. Under high pressure and heat, any rock can become coarse-grained gneiss.

This quarry is just outside Carrara in northwest Italy, a city famous for the high quality of its marble.

CHINON, FRANCE

Many towns and castles in the Loire Valley, France, have beautiful roof tiles of blue slate—it keeps out water and won't catch fire. The region is known for the purity of its slate.

METAMORPHIC MONUMENTS

Konark Sun Temple, India: Khondalite (a type of gneiss)

Christ the Redeemer, Brazil: Soapstone

Parthenon, Greece: Marble

Taj Mahal, India: White marble cladding

Washington Monument, USA: Marble

Mayan carving, Copán, Honduras

DID YOU KNOW? Renaissance artist Michelangelo used Carrara marble for his two most famous sculptures: The *Pieta* (1498-9) and *David* (1501-4.)

52

Marble forms where super-hot magma or lava heats limestone to extreme temperatures.

Common Metamorphic Rocks

MARBLE
High heat turns limestone to marble. Pure limestone forms white marble; if it has other minerals besides calcite, the marble has veins and comes in pink, green, or other hues.

ECLOGITE
If basalt or gabbro come under great pressure and heat, they form eclogite. This rock has chunks of red garnet in a matrix (background of finer-grained rock) of green omphacite.

GNEISS
Any rock can metamorphose into gneiss under high heat and pressure. The minerals separate out into bands. The lighter bands are usually feldspar and quartz.

The ancient Romans built the Pantheon and Trajan's Column in Rome, Italy, using Carrara marble. It was also the building material for Marble Arch in London, UK.

Quarry workers use diamond drills and cables to cut away huge blocks of marble. Each block weighs up to 11,300 kg (25,000 lb).

Minerals

Rocks are made up of minerals—solids that naturally grow underground or in water. We mine (dig up) minerals to extract useful elements (pure, basic substances). Diamond is an example of a mineral that is just one element.

It's Elemental!

Most minerals are compounds—mixtures of elements. Sulfides are minerals formed when metals or metal-like elements combine with sulfur; silicates form when metals combine with silicon and oxygen. Minerals or rocks that contain useful minerals are called ores.

Jade is the common name for two different minerals—jadeite and nephrite. East Asian artists have worked with both since ancient times.

Nephrite is the most common jade. When it's creamy white, it is nicknamed "mutton fat" jade. It also comes in pale green, red, yellow, lavender, black, and white.

Cinnabar is the most common ore of the metal mercury. It is the natural form of mercury sulfide.

Galena is the most common ore of the metal lead. It is the natural form of lead sulfide and sometimes also contains silver.

MOST COMMON MINERALS IN EARTH'S CRUST		
1. Feldspar	6. Calcite	
2. Quartz	7. Magnetite	
3. Olivine	8. Hematite	
4. White mica	9. Pyroxene	
5. Black mica	10. Amphibole	

Feldspar makes up around 60 percent of land rocks.

The drill is operated with a foot treadle so the craftworker can hold the piece in both hands.

A mix of water and sand drips onto the jade as it's carved, giving a smooth finish.

Useful Minerals

Many everyday essentials are made from minerals, including copper pipes and wires, lithium batteries, quartz clocks, and silicon chips. We use minerals in our foods, medicines, machines, cleaning products, replacement body parts, and much more!

Silica, found in quartz, is the main ingredient for glass. This glassblower added cadmium, selenium, and sulfur to the glass to turn it orange.

DID YOU KNOW? Around 600 compound minerals are sulfides, and around 500 are silicates.

Crystals

If it has enough room, a mineral will grow into a regular, geometrical shape called a crystal. Its molecules stick together in a particular pattern.

The Cave of Crystals in Mexico contains some of the largest natural crystals ever found.

Common Crystal

Quartz is one of the most common crystals. It can be clear or, if it contains trace minerals or impurities, take other forms—amethyst is purple quartz, citrine is yellow, and rose quartz is milky pink, for example. The basic quartz molecule has four oxygen atoms and one silicon. So long as nothing else gets in the way, quartz molecules grow to form six-sided prisms.

As these clear quartz crystals formed, they trapped the needle–shaped crystals of another mineral, rutile.

AMAZING CRYSTALS

Alexandrite: Changes from red to green to yellow in different lights

Autunite: Fluoresces under ultraviolet (UV) light

Fluorite: Different varieties come in many hues

Red beryl: A red gemstone far rarer than rubies

Autunite

56

It probably took at least half a million years for these crystals to form. They started to grow when gypsum on the cave floor was heated by magma in a chamber 3–5 km (2–3 miles) below.

Crystal Systems

VESUVIANITE

CUBIC
A 6–, 8–, or 12–sided prism on a square base

PYRITE

TETRAGONAL
A rectangular prism on a square base

SULFUR

HEXAGONAL/TRIGONAL
Two crystal systems (of 6– or 3–sided shapes) that form one crystal family

TITANIUM QUARTZ

ORTHORHOMBIC
A flattened rectangular prism shape

MONOCLINIC
A rectangular prism on a parallelogram base

CHALCANTHITE

TRICLINIC
The most irregular crystal shape with the least symmetry

EPIDOTE

Geologists exploring the cave wore protective suits because it was so hot—up to 58°C (136°F)—and humid.

Water originally filled this cave but was pumped out by miners working above. Today the cave is reflooded, because exposure to air was damaging the crystals.

DID YOU KNOW? The largest crystal discovered in the Cave of Crystals was 12 m (39 ft) long, 4 m (13 ft) wide, and weighed 50 tonnes (55 tons).

57

Metals

Metals are solids that are usually hard and shiny. They melt when they are heated and they're malleable (can be hammered into new shapes). Some metals, such as silver, copper, platinum, zinc, iron, and mercury are made of "native element minerals"—minerals that are made of a single element.

Pure or Ore?

Metals and alloys (mixes of two or more metals) sometimes occur as nuggets, grains, or veins in the rock. More often, metals are found in ores, chemically bonded to other elements. We extract metals from ores by smelting (heating to high temperatures.)

Bolivia's Cerro Rico ("rich mountain"), near the city of Potosí, has one of the world's largest silver and tin mines.

Miners blast at the underground rock with explosives, then load the resulting rubble onto mine train carts. These carry the silver ore to the surface.

These gold crystals fan out like the branches of a tree. If they had unlimited space and weren't in a narrow vein in the quartz, the crystals would be cubic.

Transporting platinum ore, South Africa

METAL PRODUCTION

Plus the nation that produces the largest share of each

Gold: 3,200 tonnes (3,500 tons)—China, 13 percent

Copper: 5.3 million tonnes (5.8 million tons)—Chile, 27 percent

Silver: 6,108 tonnes (6,733 tons)—Mexico, 16 percent

Tin: 125,000 tonnes (137,800 tons)—China, 42 percent

Platinum: 110,000 tonnes (121,000 tons)—South Africa, 68 percent

DID YOU KNOW? Mercury is the only metal that is liquid at room temperature.

It's rare to find a pure silver nugget. Silver is usually found in ores such as argentite (silver and sulfur), galena (silver and lead), or chlorargyrite (silver and chlorine).

The only light in the 1 m/3.3 ft–wide tunnel comes from the miners' headlamps.

Using Metals

People learned to extract copper 10,000 years ago. By 3,000 years ago we were adding tin to make bronze, an alloy that was stronger than copper or tin. We could extract and work iron—a process that requires much higher temperatures—from around 1,200 years ago.

This electromagnetic crane is separating out iron from other scrap so it can be reused. Only a few metals are magnetic—iron, nickel, cobalt, and some alloys.

Gemstones

Some crystals are so beautiful that we wear them as jewels. Diamonds, rubies, sapphires, and emeralds are all gemstones. We also use some rocks as gems, such as lapis lazuli.

Cut and Polish

Very few gemstones are used in their natural form—they are cut to make the most of their beauty. Giving a jewel facets (flat, angled "windows") makes it extra sparkly. Smoothing it into a rounded dome called a cabochon shows off patterns in the stone.

The Imperial State Crown is part of a collection of jewels belonging to the British monarch. It's decorated with 2,901 gemstones.

A "raw" opal (left) has not been cut or polished. Cut as a cabochon (right) the opal flashes blue, green, and other hues.

Organic Gems

Some gems aren't minerals at all! Clear, golden amber is the fossilized sap of prehistoric trees; shiny, black jet is a form of coal, made from ancient tree trunks. Pearls and coral are organic jewels from the sea.

If an irritating grain of sand gets stuck in its shell, an oyster coats it in a shimmering substance called nacre. The nacre layers build up to form a pearl.

This sapphire has belonged to kings and queens of England for nearly 1,000 years.

The Black Prince's Ruby at the front of the crown is actually a red spinel, not a ruby.

We measure gemstones in carats. One carat is 200 mg (0.007 oz).

The ingredients in red spinel are magnesia, iron, oxygen, and chromium. The highest quality of red spinel is rarer than ruby, though it is less expensive.

This enormous, 317-carat diamond is called the Cullinan II. It has 66 facets.

LARGEST GEMSTONES

1,700,000 carats: Bahia Emerald

22,892 carats: American Golden Topaz (yellow topaz)

1,404 carats: Star of Adam (star sapphire)

1,370 carats: Neelanjali Ruby (double-star ruby)

546 carats: Golden Jubilee Diamond

An emerald mined at Bahia, Brazil

DID YOU KNOW? The Black Prince's Ruby was one of the jewels that decorated the battle helmet worn by Henry V, king of England from 1413 to 1422.

Fossils

The rocks of our planet are like a history book. Paleontologists study fossils—animals and plants preserved in rock—to find out about the past. Archaeologists specialize in the story of humankind. They dig up human remains and artifacts.

Preserved in Rock

If plant or animal remains sink down into sediment or are trapped in volcanic lava or ash, their hard parts fossilize (turn to rock.) The process can take millions of years. Ancient objects are found preserved in the ground, too—from tools to treasure troves, and from buildings to boats.

These are the fossilized remains of an extinct animal called a trilobite. The oceans were home to trilobites from 520 to 250 mya.

Most of the rock at Atapuerca is sedimentary chert, sandstone, and limestone. There is also quartzite, a metamorphic rock.

FAMOUS FOSSIL BEDS

Auca Mahuevo, Argentina: Titanosaur nesting site, 83–79 mya

La Brea Tar Pits, USA: Ice Age animals, 20,000 to 10,000 ya

Smilodon skull, La Brea, USA

Liaoning, China: Feathered dinosaurs, 133–120 mya

Olduvai Gorge, Tanzania: Early humans, from 1.9 mya

Riversleigh, Australia: Megafauna from 25 mya

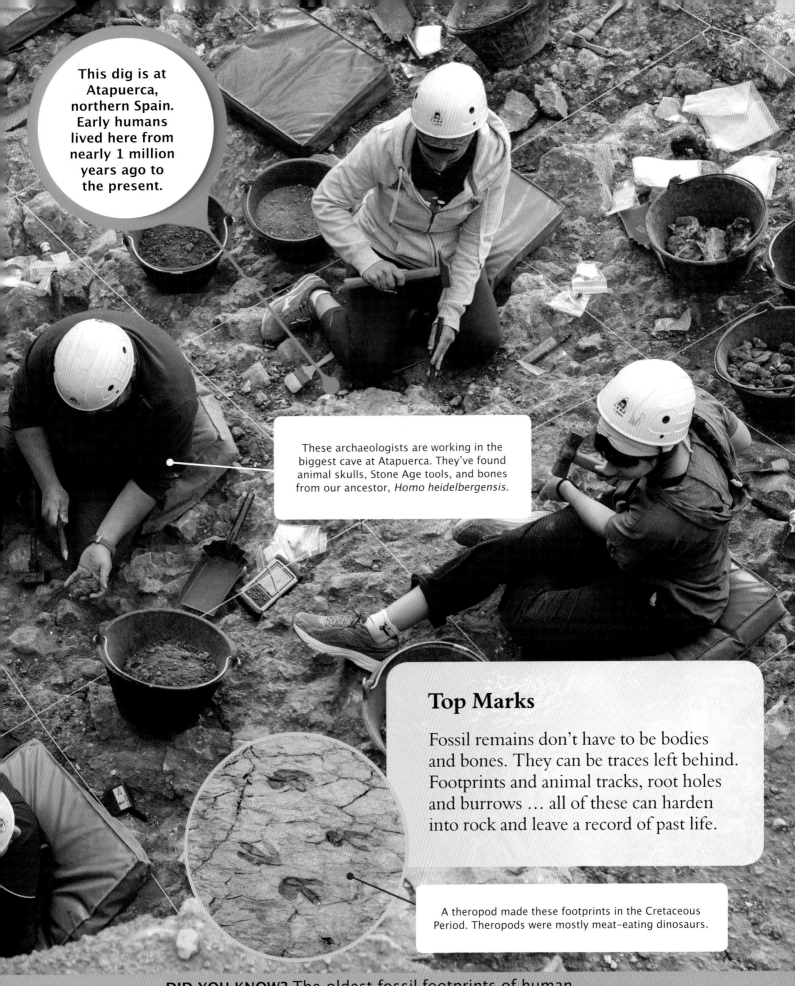

This dig is at Atapuerca, northern Spain. Early humans lived here from nearly 1 million years ago to the present.

These archaeologists are working in the biggest cave at Atapuerca. They've found animal skulls, Stone Age tools, and bones from our ancestor, *Homo heidelbergensis*.

Top Marks

Fossil remains don't have to be bodies and bones. They can be traces left behind. Footprints and animal tracks, root holes and burrows ... all of these can harden into rock and leave a record of past life.

A theropod made these footprints in the Cretaceous Period. Theropods were mostly meat-eating dinosaurs.

DID YOU KNOW? The oldest fossil footprints of human ancestors found are in Tanzania and date back 3.7 mya.

Fossil Fuels

Coal, petroleum (oil), and natural gas are cheap, reliable, and provide more than two-thirds of the world's energy. However, combusting (burning) them is a major cause of global warming because it gives off carbon dioxide.

Forming Fuel

Fossil fuels are the remains of plants and animals. The story of coal begins in prehistoric, swampy forests. Mud or acidic water broke down fallen tree trunks, creating peat bogs. Over millions of years, sediment buried the peat, pressing it to make seams of coal. Petroleum (oil) and natural gas formed in a similar way from the bodies of animals and plants that sank into sediment on the seabed.

The natural form of petroleum (oil) is crude oil. Before we can use it, it has to be processed in a refinery, such as this one at Wakayama, Japan.

Over long distances, boats or trains transport coal, while pipes carry petroleum (oil) and natural gas. Large trucks move fossil fuels over short distances.

From lightest to heaviest, the refined oil produces bottled gas and fuel for cars, aircraft, trucks, central heating, and power stations.

Sticky bitumen (tar) is left behind after the oil has been refined into different fuels. We use tar to waterproof roads and roofs.

DID YOU KNOW? Anthracite is the best–quality coal. It is a metamorphic rock, formed when sedimentary coal comes under huge heat and pressure.

Precious Peat

Peat bogs are "carbon sinks"—they absorb harmful carbon dioxide from the atmosphere. These wetlands are also a unique habitat for rare plants and animals. Unfortunately, many bogs have been drained for grazing or harvested for their peat.

The crude oil is heated to 400°C (750°F). It divides into different fuels that settle at particular levels in the "fractionating tower."

In some parts of the world, peat is burned as a fuel. It is also sold to gardeners as turf.

This unit stores liquefied petroleum gas (LPG), or bottled gas.

LARGEST REFINERIES

Daily processing capacity.
One barrel = 159 l (42 US gallons)

1,240,000 barrels: Jamnagar Refinery, Gujarat, India

940,000 barrels: Paraguana Refinery, Falcón, Venezuela

850,000 barrels: SK Energy Refinery, Ulsan, South Korea

817,000 barrels: Ruwais Refinery, Ruwais, UAE

730,000 barrels: Yeosu Refinery, South Korea

Yeosu, South Korea

Water

When you look at Planet Earth from outer space, it looks blue. This is because 71 percent of our planet is covered in water. Water is essential to keep animals, plants, and humans alive. As well as water for drinking, we need it for use in our homes, for industry, and for farmers growing food.

Solid, Liquid, Gas

Water is an unusual chemical because it can be a solid, liquid, or gas within the normal range of temperatures found on Earth. Over the course of a year, a body of water may freeze, melt, and evaporate.

Trees and other plants are dependent on water. They, in turn, provide food and homes for wildlife.

As water travels down mountains or hills, it can plunge over a ridge of hard rock, creating a waterfall. Over thousands of years, the water erodes or wears away the rocks.

Scientists have discovered and documented 230,000 water-dwelling species—including seven types of sea turtle.

WORLD'S HIGHEST WATERFALLS

1. **Angel Falls, Venezuela:** 979 m (3,212 ft)
2. **Tugela Falls, South Africa:** 948 m (3,110 ft)
3. **Tres Hermanas Falls, Peru:** 914 m (2,999 ft)
4. **Olo'upena Falls, Hawaii:** 900 m (2,953 ft)

Angel Falls

DID YOU KNOW? Less than 1% of the water on Earth can be used as drinking water.

The Water Cycle

The sun heats the surface of areas of water such as oceans and rivers. As the water warms, it evaporates. The evaporated water cools as it rises through the air, turns into water droplets, and forms clouds. When the droplets get too big, the water falls back to Earth as rain, snow, sleet, or hail.

1. Water from rivers and oceans evaporates into the air.
2. It turns into cloud.
3. Heavy clouds turn into rain.
4. Rain falls into rivers and oceans.

Water cascades over the rocks into a plunge pool. The clear, cool water is home to wildlife and provides drinking water for animals and birds.

The water in oceans is salty but most of the water away from oceans and coasts is freshwater.

Rivers and Lakes

The rain that falls on the land gradually runs into inland waterways such as rivers, lakes, streams, and reservoirs. These freshwater sources give us the clean water we need every day for drinking, cooking, and cleaning, and to grow food. Just 2.5% of the water on Earth is fresh—the rest is saltwater, which cannot be used in these ways.

People and Rivers

In many countries, fish from rivers and lakes is an important source of food for the local communities. People use boats to travel from one place to another and to transport goods. Water from local freshwater sources is used to water crops.

For Hindus, the Ganges River in India is sacred. They visit the river to pray and bathe, and the ashes of the dead are scattered into its waters.

Types of Lake

Lakes form in many ways. The Great Lakes of North America formed during the Ice Age, when ice sheets carved deep holes into the ground. As the ice melted, the holes filled with the melted water and became glacial lakes.

Lake Baikal lies in a rift valley where the Earth's crust is slowly pulling apart, creating a trench that is filled with water.

Glaciers tower above Lake Argentino, part of the Los Glaciares National Park in Argentina. Chunks of ice break off the glacier and form ice floes on the lake.

Cranberries are planted in peat bogs. At harvest time the bogs are flooded with water. The berries rise to the top of the water to be picked.

DID YOU KNOW? Lake Baikal in Russia is the world's oldest, largest and deepest lake. It is home to the nerpa, the world's only freshwater seals.

The Yangtze River is the largest in China. One third of Chinese people live in its river basin.

River fishing has provided a livelihood for local people for generations. Tourist cruises are also a source of income.

The Mississippi River

WORLD'S LONGEST RIVERS

1. **Amazon, South America:** 6,990 km (4,260 miles)
2. **Nile, Africa:** 6,850 km (4,255 miles)
3. **Yangtze, China:** 6,300 km (3,920 miles)
4. **Mississippi, United States:** 6,275 km (3,900 miles)

Oceans

Oceans cover more than 70 percent of the Earth's surface. They are home to millions of species of plants and animals. The oceans are a vital source of food and water for humans as well as providing a transport route for people and goods around the world. We are only just beginning to explore the deepest parts of the ocean.

A baby shark hunts for food. Sharks are top predators in the ocean food chain.

Climate Controller

The ocean plays an important role in keeping Earth's climate stable, because it absorbs a huge amount of heat in the summer, then releases it in the winter. This makes the Earth warmer in winter and cooler in summer.

Huge freight ships carry cargo such as furniture, food, and cars around the world. They can carry thousands of tons of cargo stacked high in special containers.

Ocean Zones

The ocean is divided into five layers called zones.

1. Sunlight or Epipelagic Zone
   200m (656 ft)

2. Twilight or Mesopelagic Zone
   1,000 m (3,281 ft)

3. Dark or Bathypelagic Zone
   4,000 m (13,124 ft)

4. The Abyss or Abyssopelagic Zone
   19, 686 ft (6,000 m)

5. The Trenches or Hadopelagic Zone
   10, 911 m (35,797 ft)

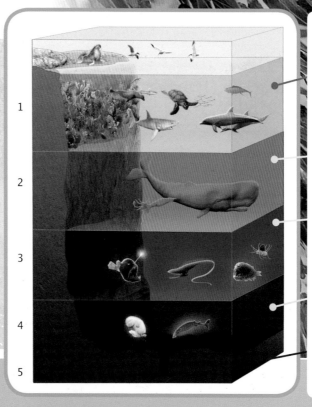

In the Sunlight Zone, the water is warm and there is light for plants and animals. It is filled with life such as fish, turtles, dolphins, and coral reefs.

The Twilight Zone has low levels of sunlight. Huge blue whales and squid are some of the animals that live here.

The Dark Zone has no sunlight. Most of the animals in this zone are red or black.

In the Abyss, there is no light, the water is cold, and the water pressure is high. Some animals that live here create their own light called bioluminescence.

The temperature in the Trenches, is near freezing, and very little lives here.

A shoal or school of fish can contain thousands of individuals. They often move in the same direction all together, creating amazing patterns. Scientists are not sure why or how they do this.

Some fish have a silvery skin so they are not easy to see in the water.

WORLD'S LARGEST OCEANS

1. **Pacific Ocean:** 165,250,000 sq km (63,800,000 sq miles)
2. **Atlantic:** 106,460,000 sq km (41,100,000 sq miles)
3. **Indian:** 70,560,000 sq km (27,240,000 sq miles)
4. **Southern:** 21,960,000 sq km (71,800,000 sq miles)
5. **Arctic:** 14,056,000 sq km (5,427,000 sq miles)

Atlantic Ocean

DID YOU KNOW? The world's largest coral reef, the Great Barrier Reef in Australia, is visible from outer space.

Waves and Currents

Waves pounding against the rocks cause them to erode and change shape.

The ocean is always moving because of waves and currents. Waves are made by the wind as it blows over the surface of the water. Waves can start a long way out to sea. As the waves get closer to the shore, the water slows down and the wave curves over and breaks.

On the Move

Ocean currents are a seasonal movement of water over large distances. They are shaped by factors such as the wind, tides, and temperature differences.

This shows the world's ocean currents. The red are warm currents and the blue are cold currents. These currents affect weather patterns around the world.

WORLD'S TALLEST WAVES

1. **Alaska:** 30 m (100 ft)
2. **Norway:** 25 m (84 ft)
3. **Portugal:** 24 m (50 ft)
4. **Hawaii:** 9 m (30 ft)

Alaska

Over many thousands of years, the constant erosion of coastal rocks by waves reshapes the shoreline.

Ocean Tides

Twice a day, ocean levels rise and cover the shore, then the level goes down and the ocean leaves the shore. These are called tides. They are caused by the Moon's gravity pulling on Earth's oceans.

SPRING TIDE

SUN

KEY

1

2

EARTH

3

NEAP TIDE

4

1. FULL MOON

2. NEW MOON

3. WAXING MOON

4. WANING MOON

Spring tides have nothing to do with the season, and take place twice a month—when the Moon is full and when it is new. At these times, the Sun and Moon are in line with the Earth, and their gravity pulls in the same direction. The result is tides that are very high or very low as the oceans "spring" out and back.

At neap tides, which take place in the first and last quarter, the Sun and the Moon are at right angles to each other, which means that the pull of the sun partially cancels out the pull of the Moon. High tides are lower, and low tides are higher.

DID YOU KNOW? Waves more than 245 m (800 ft) tall can form and break under the water in the deepest parts of the ocean.

Weather Systems

All weather is driven by the uneven way that the Sun heats the atmosphere, land, and oceans. This causes air masses to move about. A big mass of air that has a steady temperature will bring steady weather. Global winds, ocean currents, the cold air around mountain ranges, and other geographical features on the ground all affect the weather.

Weather Fronts

A warm front is the point where a warm air mass meets a colder air mass and moves up and over the colder air. A cold front is where a colder air mass advances into and pushes up a warm air mass.

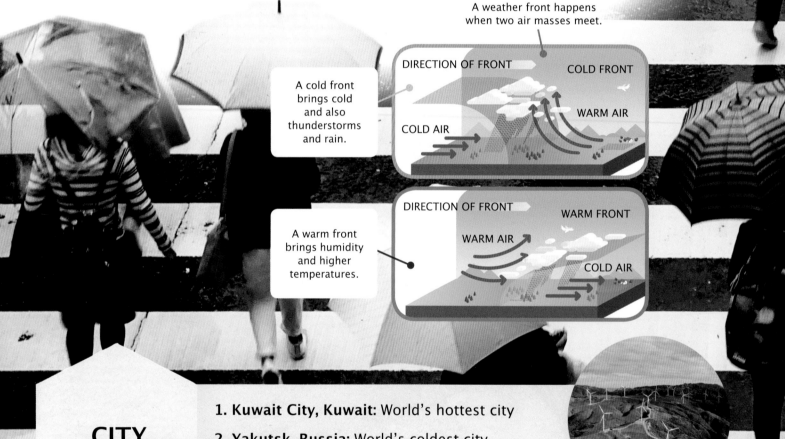

A weather front happens when two air masses meet.

A cold front brings cold and also thunderstorms and rain.

DIRECTION OF FRONT
COLD FRONT
WARM AIR
COLD AIR

A warm front brings humidity and higher temperatures.

DIRECTION OF FRONT
WARM FRONT
WARM AIR
COLD AIR

CITY WEATHER EXTREMES

1. **Kuwait City, Kuwait:** World's hottest city
2. **Yakutsk, Russia:** World's coldest city
3. **Aswan, Egypt:** World's driest city
4. **Buenaventura, Colombia:** World's wettest city
5. **Wellington, New Zealand:** World's windiest city

Wind farm in Wellington, New Zealand

DID YOU KNOW? Other planets with atmospheres have winds. Neptune has the highest wind speeds of 2,092 km/h (1,300 mph).

Weather forecasting helps us prepare for whatever weather is to come.

Wind

Wind is the movement of air. Wind happens when there is a difference in temperature in the Earth's atmosphere. Warm air is lighter than cool air, so it rises higher above the Earth. Cool air rushes into the space where the warm air once was.

NORTH POLE

EQUATOR

SOUTH POLE

Most countries around the world have rain of some kind at some time during the year, even deserts.

Wind is also created by the spin of the Earth and the difference in temperature between the equator and polar areas. Global winds carry warm air around the Earth.

Storms and Precipitation

When water freezes in clouds it forms tiny flat six-sided crystals. These crystals join together to make snowflakes. No two snowflakes look the same.

Rain, snow, and hail are all forms of precipitation. When the air cools, moisture forms into tiny, floating droplets, which we call clouds. The droplets collect into bigger drops, until they're too heavy to stay aloft—then they fall as rain. In cold weather, the moisture turns into crystals, and forms snow or hail instead.

Thunder and Lightning

During a thunderstorm you will hear thunder and see lightning and (usually) heavy rain. Thunderstorms develop in tall, dark cumulonimbus clouds. Ice and water particles bump into each other inside the cloud, building up an electric charge. When the negative charge in the cloud connects to a positive charge on the ground or elsewhere in the cloud, we see an electrical spark—lightning! Thunder is caused by the lightning, and can be a loud crack or a low rumble.

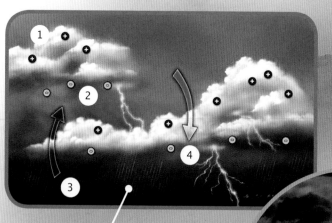

Inside a thundercloud, frozen raindrops collide with each other, creating an electric charge. (1) Positive charges (protons) collect at the top of the cloud and (2) negative charges (electrons) collect at the bottom, nearer to the ground.

(3) Opposites attract, so when a positive charge builds up on the ground, (4) it connects to a negative charge reaching down from the cloud, and lightning strikes.

Lightning makes a hole in the air called a channel. Thunder is the sound of the hole collapsing when the lightning has gone.

WORLD'S LARGEST HAILSTONE

In June 2003, the world's largest hailstone fell in Aurora, Nebraska. It was 18 cm (7 in) across and about 48 cm (19 in) in circumference.

World's largest hailstone

DID YOU KNOW? You can hear thunder up to 24 km (15 miles) away and you can see lightning up to 161 km (100 miles) away!

During a blizzard visibility is greatly reduced so you cannot see very far ahead.

Types of Clouds

Different cloud types form in different weather conditions. Some clouds form close to the ground, others high in the sky. We can predict the weather by looking at cloud shapes and how high in the sky they are.

A blizzard is a long-lasting heavy snow storm with very strong winds. Blizzards happen when warm air rises over very cold or freezing air near the ground.

1. Altocumulus is a mid-level cloud.
2. Nimbostratus clouds can bring rain.
3. Cumulonimbus clouds bring heavy rain and storms.
4. Fluffy cumulus clouds form at low levels.

Floods and Drought

In Thailand, a volunteer boat rescues property and pets from a flood.

Heavy rain can cause rivers and lakes to overflow, so that water floods the land. In India and tropical parts of Southeast Asia, heavy rains called monsoons can flood the streets but they also provide much-needed water for crops. If the floods are severe, they can damage crops and homes and be a danger to people and animals.

Flood Barriers

Levees are raised walls or banks used to stop rivers overflowing. Dams are huge barriers built to control the flow of water, and usually any excess water is collected in a reservoir or lake. Floodways are channels that divert water away from overflowing rivers or lakes.

The world's largest movable storm barrier protects the low–lying Netherlands from floods. The storm gates are usually open but swing together to form a barrier to stop flood waters.

WORLD'S HEAVIEST RAINFALL

Monsoons in Cherrapunji in India make it one of the wettest places on Earth with the heaviest rainfall. In 1995, 1,563 mm (62 in) of rain fell in one day.

Cherrapunji

DID YOU KNOW? More people drown in the desert than die of thirst. Sudden, heavy rain causes flash floods because the sand doesn't soak up the water quickly enough.

The monsoon season lasts from June to September and can have devastating effects. Sometimes thousands of people are killed and millions made homeless.

Flood water can cause serious health risks if it is contaminated with human waste, garbage, or chemicals from factories.

Drought and Famine

A drought happens when there is not enough rain. Rivers and streams that supply drinking water dry up. Crops fail because farmers cannot irrigate the land. If there is not enough water or food for livestock, they may die too. This leads to famine.

Reservoirs are big artificial lakes of water. This one has dried up, leaving the earth cracked and parched.

Tornadoes

Tornadoes form when certain types of weather collide. When warm and humid air near the ground meets colder air above, it punches through the cold layer and storm clouds develop. Winds blowing through the clouds twist the rising air currents, forming a whirlwind. The whirlwind spins faster and faster until it becomes a fierce tornado.

Danger Ahead!

As the tornado swirls across the land, it picks up any objects in its path and can carry them a long distance. Most tornadoes happen in the United States, in the Great Plains, in an area known as Tornado Alley.

Tornadoes connect the clouds and the ground. They are also called twisters or cyclones.

A very strong tornado can pick up cars and houses and destroy everything in its path.

Tornadoes are measured using the Fujita Scale or F-Scale. The scale ranges from F0 to F5, the strongest and most destructive type of tornadoes.

WORLD'S WORST TORNADO

In 1925, one of the largest and fastest tornadoes in U.S. history raged for 354 km (220 miles) across the states of Missouri, Illinois, and Indiana. It killed 689 people.

Map of the tornado's path

DID YOU KNOW? The fastest winds on Earth occur inside tornadoes where wind speeds can reach 402 km/h (250 mph).

A tornado is a column of twisting air that picks up dust and other debris as it travels across the land.

The base of a tornado can be up to 4 km (2.6 miles) wide, though they're usually much smaller. Some tornadoes last for hours, and others can blow out after only a few minutes.

Tornado Chasers

Storm chasers are people who follow tornadoes as they travel across the land. Most storm chasers do it for the excitement and to take photographs and videos. Some scientists do it to find out more about tornadoes.

Doppler radar on top of a truck can pick up weather signs showing the start of a tornado.

Hurricanes

Hurricanes are powerful, swirling storms also known as tropical cyclones. They begin out at sea and can travel across the water to reach land, where they cause devastation. Strong winds and dark clouds rotate on the outside of a hurricane. The middle, called the eye of the storm, is usually calm and cloudless.

Hurricane Havoc

Hurricane winds can reach up to 252 km/h (157 mph) as the warm air spirals around the storm system. A hurricane can also raise the sea level beneath it, causing floods that threaten lives, destroy houses, and damage crops.

When a hurricane strikes, homes are evacuated and people gather in a place of safety. Many are left homeless.

Most hurricanes form in late summer when sea temperatures are at their highest.

The Beaufort Scale measures the force of wind based on speed and the effect it has on its surroundings. There are 13 levels.

0	1	2	3	4	5	6
Speed: less than 1 km/h (1 mph). Calm. Smoke rises vertically.	Speed: 1–5 km/h (1–3 mph). Light air. Smoke drifts in the direction of the wind.	Speed: 6–11 km/h (4–7 mph). Light breeze. Wind felt on face; leaves rustle.	Speed: 12–19 km/h (8–12 mph). Gentle breeze. Leaves and small twigs constantly moving.	Speed: 20–28 km/h (13–18 mph). Moderate breeze. Raises dust and loose paper; small branches moved.	Speed: 29–38 km/h (19–24 mph). Fresh breeze. Small trees with leaves begin to sway. Small crested waves on inland water.	Speed: 38–49 km/h (25–31 mph). Strong breeze. Large branches moved. Umbrellas used with difficulty.

WORLD'S WORST HURRICANE

The worst hurricane in recent history happened in 1998. Hurricane Mitch struck South America, moving through Belize, El Salvador, Guatemala, Honduras, and Nicaragua. Rainfall caused flash floods and mudslides. More than 11,000 people died, roads were destroyed, and millions of people became homeless.

Hurricane Mitch

How Hurricanes Form

Hurricanes form over warm water when different weather systems come together (1). They all rotate and swirl into one giant spiral (2). Warm, moist air rises on the edges of the storm. (3) Dry air sinks through the eye of the storm.

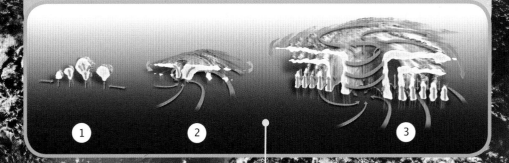

1   2   3

Inward flowing winds, low pressure at the core of the storm, and rain are all features of a hurricane.

Huge cumulonimbus clouds tower up into the atmosphere, causing heavy rain and lightning.

Speed: 50–61 km/h (32–38 mph). Near gale. Whole trees moved. Difficulty walking against the wind.

Speed: 62–74 km/h (39–46 mph). Gale. Twigs break off trees. Difficult to walk.

Speed: 75–88 km/h (47–54 mph). Strong gale. Chimney pots and roof slates might be damaged.

Speed: 89–102 km/h (55–63 mph). Storm. Trees uprooted; serious damage to buildings.

Speed: 103–117 km/h (64–72 mph). Violent storm. Widespread damage.

Speed: 118 plus km/h (73 plus mph). Hurricane. Devastation.

7   8   9   10   11   12

Weather Forecasting

The JPSS is in polar orbit, circling the Earth from the North Pole to the South Pole.

Meteorology is the science of predicting the weather. Meteorologists collect data from many different sources such as weather stations, high-altitude balloons, and satellites. There are thousands of weather stations around the world, which collect information by measuring rainfall, hours of sunshine, temperature, air pressure, wind speed, and facts about the weather in that area.

Weather Data

Data is fed into computers that predict weather patterns. The predictions can be reasonably accurate for up to a week, but weather patterns change constantly. Weather forecasts are useful for farmers and sailors, who need to be prepared for weather changes.

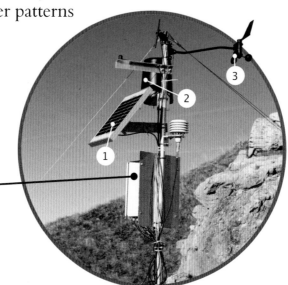

This weather station has a solar panel (1) to measure hours of sunshine, a rain gauge (2), and an anemometer (3) that measures wind speed and directions.

Instruments attached to a weather balloon record data such as humidity, wind speed, and temperature.

The JPSS has five sensors that will collect data about conditions over land and sea.

JOINT POLAR SATELLITE SYSTEM

The JPSS-1 spacecraft orbits the globe 14 times a day (every 90 minutes) from one pole to the other at an 824 km (512 miles) elevation above the surface of Earth—providing scientists full coverage of the planet twice a day.

Weather satellite in orbit

Life Saver

The Joint Polar Satellite System (JPSS) is the latest technology being used in space to monitor extreme weather conditions and climate change. The data it collects will allow scientists to predict the arrival of dangerous weather systems such as hurricanes.

Weather maps use lines and arrows to show the different weather fronts that are expected.

Data collected from the JPSS will be sent to weather forecasters and scientists to help them monitor changes in the Earth's atmosphere.

DID YOU KNOW? The first radio weather forecasts were broadcast in the United States in 1925.

85

Climate Zones

The brown bear is found in the boreal forests of northern North America and Eurasia. In winter, its fur is very thick and long, up to 12 cm (5 in).

Climate is the general weather in a place over time, such as the temperature and how much rain falls. The three basic climates are tropical (near the equator), polar (around the poles), and temperate (everything in between). A biome is a group of habitats that share a similar climate.

A Rough Guide

Differences in temperature, light, and rainfall across the seasons create different biomes. Boreal forests are found south of the Arctic, while rain forests are typical in tropical climates. Biomes don't have clear borders, though—but slowly change from one to another.

TEMPERATE BROADLEAF FOREST

CONIFEROUS FOREST

TEMPERATE GRASSLAND

MEDITERRANEAN

TROPICAL RAIN FOREST

DESERT

MOUNTAIN

TUNDRA

POLAR

On this map, the world's land is divided into nine biomes that share similar climates. Each biome can be subdivided into even more precise biomes.

BOREAL FORESTS

Area: 200,000 sq km (77,220 sq miles)

Locations: Canada, Russia, Scandinavia

Temperature Range: -54°C to 21°C (-65°F to 70°F)

Trees: Spruce, fir, pine, and deciduous larch

Mammals: Bear, wolf, lynx, caribou, moose, beaver, weasel

Altai Mountains, Siberia, Russia

Underwater Biomes

Rivers, lakes, ponds, streams, and many wetlands are all freshwater biomes. Marine, or saltwater, biomes range from estuaries, coastal areas, and coral reefs to the different depths of the pelagic zone (open ocean). Each biome has its own conditions.

Most trees in boreal forests are conifers. Instead of flat leaves, they have thin needles that help to save water. Their branches slope downward so snow can fall off.

Shallow-water coral reefs, like this one in the Red Sea, teem with life.

Brown bear cubs stay with their mother for around two and a half years. After that, they must fend for themselves.

Tough bracken ferns die back in winter but survive and cover the forest floor in summer.

DID YOU KNOW? The Russian boreal forests, or "taiga," are rich in insects during the breeding season, so many birds nest here, including wood warblers.

Climate Change

Climate change is nothing new! In the last 650,000 years, the Earth has had seven periods of cooling during which glaciers have advanced—and then retreated as the temperature has risen. The difference now is that human activity is driving the change. Since 1880, Earth's average surface temperature has risen by 0.8°C (1.4°F).

Human Activity

One key cause of climate change is the burning of fossil fuels such as coal, gas, and oil. This releases carbon dioxide (CO_2) into the air, which traps heat from the Sun, warming the Earth—the so-called Greenhouse Effect.

Trees absorb CO_2 and so are vital to keep the planet healthy. Yet huge areas of forests, such as this one in Borneo, are cut down to make way for crop and cattle farms.

Rising Sea Levels

Experts predict sea levels will rise 0.3 m–2.5 m (1 ft–8.2 ft) during the next century due to global warming. This is partly because water expands as its temperature rises. Melting glaciers and polar ice are also adding extra water into the oceans.

If sea levels continue to rise, many of the 1,192 low-lying coral islands that make up the Maldives in southern Asia will be underwater some time this century.

CLIMATE CHANGE IN FIGURES

32 percent: Increase in CO_2 emissions between 1760 and 2018

2016: The year Bhutan became the first country to produce less CO_2 than its plant life absorbs

87 percent: The proportion of CO_2 produced by human activity that is caused by burning fossil fuels (coal, oil, and natural gas)

73,000 sq km (28,000 sq miles): Forest destroyed each year

Bhutan

Arctic sea ice is currently shrinking by 13 percent each decade.

The Arctic is warming nearly twice as fast as the rest of the world. Polar bears and seals need the Arctic ice to survive.

Polar bears depend on the sea ice environment. Melting ice forces them to travel farther to reach the seals that are their prey.

DID YOU KNOW? The Glacier National Park in Montana had over 150 glaciers in 1850. In 2018 it was down to 25. All its glaciers will eventually disappear due to global warming.

Deserts

Desert winds blow the sand into ripples, ridges, and dunes. The Sahara's sand is a distinctive reddish gold shade.

With an average of less than 250 mm (10 in) of rain a year, deserts are the driest places on Earth. Those closer to the equator, such as the Sahara, are hot year-round. Further from the equator, deserts can be cold part or all of the time. Instead of sand, some are bare rock, stripped of all soil.

Desert Animals

A desert looks lifeless, but insects, small reptiles, and mammals are active at night, hiding from the daytime heat in burrows. Special features let them benefit from any moisture—the fogstand beetle collects water on its back from early morning fogs.

A few traders still use camels to transport goods across the Sahara. However, most rely on trucks or planes.

The Arabian oryx is a desert antelope that can go for weeks without water. It can also sense rainfall from far away. Its white coat reflects the sunlight.

WORLD'S LARGEST DESERTS

1. **Antarctica:** 14.25 million sq km (5.5 million sq miles)
2. **Arctic:** 14 million sq km (5.4 million sq miles)
3. **Sahara Desert:** 9.06 million sq km (3.5 million sq miles)
4. **Arabian Desert:** 2.6 million sq km (1 million sq miles)
5. **Gobi Desert:** 1.3 million sq km (500,000 sq miles)

Antarctica

The Sahara is the largest hot and sandy desert in the world. It stretches across North Africa.

Plant Survival

Desert plants' leaves have adapted to lose very little water. They include spiky grasses, shrubs with small, scale-like leaves, and succulents that store water in thick leaves. Cacti store water in their trunk and stems. They also have thin spines instead of leaves.

The saguaro cactus is found only in the Sonoran Desert of the southwestern United States and its surrounding area. It grows more than 12 m (40 ft) tall.

Some of the Tuareg—nomads who live in the Sahara—follow a traditional way of life. They guide camel caravans, and herd goats, sheep, cattle, and camels.

Flowers carpet the desert after rare rainfall. The plants grow, flower, and seed in just a few weeks. The seeds lie dormant until the next rains.

A camel's body is adapted to keep out the sand. It has hair-lined ears, long eyelashes, and nostrils that close.

A camel's hump stores fat, not water. The fat can be used for energy when food is scarce. The camel's thick lips can cope with eating prickly desert plants.

DID YOU KNOW? Chile's Atacama Desert is the world's driest desert. Some parts of it have had no rain since weather stations were set up there.

Grasslands

Grasslands are found around the world, from the cold north to the hot tropics. Warm, tropical grasslands include the African and Australian savannahs. Temperate grasslands are cooler and wetter, such as the American Prairies, the veld in South Africa, and the South American pampas.

Grassland Animals

A wide variety of animals live in grasslands. Wild sheep clamber about in mountain grasslands while giraffes, zebra, and antelope graze on the African savannah. Huge areas of grassland are now being cleared for crops and animal farming.

In the pampas, giant anteaters sniff out termite nests. They tear them open with their sharp claws and use their long, sticky tongue to scoop out the insects.

WORLD'S LARGEST GRASSLANDS

1. **Savannah, Africa:** 12.9 million square km (5 million sq miles)

2. **Prairie, North America:** 3.6 million square km (1.4 million sq miles)

3. **Pampas, South America:** 760,000 square km (295,000 sq miles)

Pampas

4. **Steppe, Central Eurasia:** stretches 8,000 km (5,000 miles) from the mouth of the Danube almost to the Pacific

The Eurasian Steppe

This vast temperate grassland stretches for about 8,000 km (5,000 miles) across Europe and Asia, from Ukraine to Mongolia. Traditionally, people on the steppe made a living herding cattle, sheep, and goats. The horse was first domesticated and ridden here. The Steppe Route has been linking people and enabling trade since as long ago as the Stone Age.

Steppes are temperate grasslands that have warm to hot summers and cool to cold winters. Wild horses roam the Mongolian steppes.

Here, African buffalo gather at a watering hole. They are the only species of cattle never to have been domesticated.

Herds of buffalo never travel more than 20 km (12 miles) from a source of water. Where water is scarce, buffalo breed mostly in the wet season.

DID YOU KNOW? More than 70 percent of the Canadian Prairies have been converted to other uses such as agriculture and industry.

Forests

Howler monkeys make a shrieking noise that can be heard 3–5 km (2–3 miles) across the forest.

Tropical forests grow near the equator, where it is hot all year round. Temperate forests grow in areas to the north and south, which are cooler and have seasons. Boreal forests grow in the subarctic region, and are also called snow forests. Eight out of ten land species—plant and animal—live in forests.

Forest Trees

Broadleaved trees have flat, wide leaves and their seeds are inside fruits. Conifer trees grow in places with cold winters and have thin, sharp needles instead of broad leaves. These help to retain water, and can survive snow. Their seeds are inside hard, woody cones, which close when wet and open when dry.

Fast-moving forest fires destroy habitat and leave people and animals homeless. Small fires can be healthy for some forests by clearing away dead and diseased growth and allowing sunlight through.

Mountain Forests

Tropical mountain forests are home to a wide range of animals, from gorillas in Central Africa to jaguars in South America. In freezing, snowy areas or mountainous regions, trees cannot grow above a certain height, called the tree line, as it is too cold and windy for them to survive.

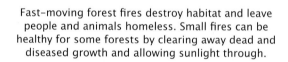

A cougar perches on a lookout point in the South American forest. Its sharp claws retract to help it climb trees and hunt.

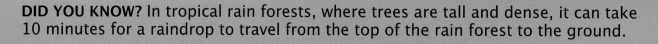

94 **DID YOU KNOW?** In tropical rain forests, where trees are tall and dense, it can take 10 minutes for a raindrop to travel from the top of the rain forest to the ground.

Monkeys, sloths, and other species use the trees to move around. Many spend all their time in the trees, and hardly ever touch the ground.

New World monkeys use their long tails as another limb, to hang onto branches as they swing through the forest.

RAIN FOREST ANIMALS IN DANGER

Eastern gorilla: Critically endangered—fewer than 5,000

Sumatran orangutan: Critically endangered—about 14,600

Javan rhinoceros: Critically endangered, less than 100

Asian elephant: Endangered—maximum 52,345

Chimpanzee: Endangered

Asian elephant

Polar Regions

With biting winds, low temperatures, and lengthy winters, life is tough at the poles. The Arctic Circle includes the Arctic Ocean, ringed by northerly North America, Europe, and Asia. The Antarctic Circle contains most of Antarctica, and the southerly waters of the Pacific, Atlantic, and Indian Oceans.

Year-Round Ice

Sea ice floats on the Arctic Ocean for most of the year. Arctic land is tundra, with permafrost (permanently frozen ground). Antarctica is mostly covered by a permanent ice sheet.

Antarctic ice is melting so fast the whole continent could collapse by the 22nd century.

Trees cannot root in the permafrost. Only small, scrubby plants survive in the tundra. They bloom briefly during the short summer.

ARCTIC ANIMALS IN DANGER

Eskimo curlew: Critically endangered (possibly extinct)

Snowy owl: Vulnerable—28,000 adult birds

Polar bear: Vulnerable—maximum 31,000 left

Walrus: Vulnerable—fewer than 225,000

Greenland shark: Near threatened—population unknown

A walrus

Herd Instincts

Reindeer or caribou travel in herds across the Arctic tundra. Each herd can consist of hundreds of individuals. As the summer starts, they begin one of the world's largest animal migrations. Some herds travel north for 1,610–2,575 km (1,000–1,600 miles) to give birth and find more abundant food.

Temperatures in Antarctica can plummet as low as –89°C (–129°F).

Caribou have two layers of fur to keep them warm. Their hair contains air pockets that act as extra insulation against the cold.

These gentoo penguins are the most northerly of the four Antarctic species. The other three are chinstrap, Adélie, and emperor penguins.

Gentoos are the fastest-swimming penguins. They zip through the icy water at 36 km/h (22 mph), catching krill and other crustaceans.

DID YOU KNOW? The Arctic is home to about four million people from more than 40 ethnic groups, including Inuit, Sami, and Nenets (Samoyeds).

Wetlands

Wetlands are habitats where water saturates the ground to form shallow pools or stretches of water. Found in every continent except Antarctica, they support a variety of wildlife. Wetlands include mangrove forests, swamps, bogs, marshes, fens— and peatlands, almost half of the world's wetlands.

Clean and Fresh

Wetlands help to control flooding. They also attract many different species of animals. However, wetland areas face serious threats from farming, building, and contamination. Some wetlands have been created deliberately, to treat water contaminated by industry.

In the Florida wetlands, alligators warm up in the sun. They are ectothermic so rely on external sources of heat to control their body temperature.

Land Meets Sea

Sandy beaches, rock pools, mangrove swamps, and coastal cliffs are habitats that are found where land meets the sea. Tidal wetlands are areas that are periodically flooded at high tides.

1. A crab scuttles along a damp, sandy beach.

2. When the tide is out, rock pools reveal amazing starfish.

3. Puffins raise their chicks on cliff edges close to the sea where they hunt for food.

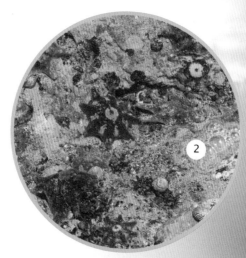

Some male herons use the trails on their caps to attract females during the mating season. They can make the trail stand upright on top of their heads.

The Cocoi heron lives in the South American wetlands. It feeds on fish, frogs, and water insects and makes its nest in bushes or reedbeds.

Aquatic plants grow on or near water. They provide cover for fish, produce oxygen, and provide food for some wildlife.

WETLANDS OF THE WORLD

Largest wetland: Pantanal (Brazil, Bolivia, and Paraguay)—up to 195,000 square km/75,000 sq miles

Largest mangrove forest: Sundarbans (Bangladesh and India)—14,000 square km/5,400 sq miles

Largest reed bed: Lower Danube and Danube delta (Bulgaria, Moldova, Romania, Serbia, and Ukraine) —5,180 square km/2,000 sq miles

Sundarbans

DID YOU KNOW? Wild rice, Chinese water chestnuts, water spinach, watercress, and Indian lotus are all aquatic plants harvested for food.

Cave Habitats

Water dripping through cracks in limestone slowly dissolves the rock. Over hundreds of years the lime in the dripping water hardens to form stalactites.

Underground caves are carved out of rock by water, often by dripping acidic groundwater that dissolves the rock. Some are worn away by underwater rivers and streams. Caves can take hundreds of thousands of years to form. Coastal caves are made by waves pounding against cliffs.

Cave Animals

Most caves are dark and damp with little or no plant life, but many animals have adapted to cave life. The adult European cave spider cannot tolerate light, while the cave swallow prefers to roost in caves or sinkholes.

Bats use echolocation to "see" in the dark. They emit sounds that bounce back. This tells them how big an object is, for example, and how far away it is.

The blind cave fish hunts by detecting small changes in the water pressure around it.

AMAZING CAVES

Longest cave system: Mammoth Cave, Kentucky, USA—at least 652 km (405 miles) long

Deepest cave: Veryovkina cave, Abkhazia, Georgia —at least 2,212 m (7,257 ft) deep

Largest underwater cave system: Sac Actun system, Yucatan, Mexico—259 km (161 miles) long

Part of the San Actun cave system, Mexico

DID YOU KNOW? Stalactites and stalagmites eventually join to make a column from ground to roof, but they only grow 0.15–1.2 mm a year.

Humans have used caves as homes, burial sites, and places of worship. Many ancient paintings have been found on cave walls.

It can take up to 100,000 years to make a cave large enough for a human.

Creating Caves

Most caves form in karst, a type of rock made of limestone, dolomite, or gypsum. Rain picks up carbon dioxide from the air and soil, making it slightly acidic. This acidic water seeps through cracks in the rock, slowly dissolving it and creating caves.

When the dripping water lands on the ground, it leaves behind minerals. Over thousands of years, these minerals grow to become stalagmites.

Farmland

A lot of natural habitats around the world, such as forests and grasslands, are disappearing to make way for farmland because demand for food is growing as the world's population increases. Arable farmers grow crops such as wheat and tend orchards for fruit. Other farmers raise herds of cows, sheep, and other animals.

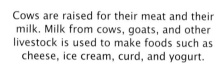

Cows are raised for their meat and their milk. Milk from cows, goats, and other livestock is used to make foods such as cheese, ice cream, curd, and yogurt.

Growing Crops

Rice is a grain that is the main food source for over half the world's population. Most of the world's rice is grown in Asia. Maize (or corn) is grown in every continent except Antarctica and is eaten as both a cereal and a vegetable. It is processed to make cooking oil and is used in lots of other foods, such as potato chips and ice cream.

Pesticides

Arable farms provide habitats for birds, small mammals, and insects. However, pesticides threaten this biodiversity—what kills insect pests may also kill the animals that eat them. Chemical fertilizers also threaten wildlife. Running off the soil into waterways, they endanger aquatic creatures.

Barns owls hunt small mammals in arable fields. Other birds nest and raise their young in the hedgerows that border fields.

WORLD'S BIGGEST CROPS

1. **Maize:** 1.07 billion tonnes (1.8 billion tons)
2. **Wheat:** 760 million tonnes (840 million tons)
3. **Rice:** 700 million tonnes (772 million tons)
4. **Potatoes:** 380 million tonnes (420 million tons)

Harvesting maize in the USA

Rice is a type of grass and needs a lot of clean, fresh water to grow. Rice fields are also called paddy fields.

Rice is usually grown in a flat field. Rice grown on a terrace like this cannot be harvested by machine, so a large, human workforce is required.

These women in traditional dress are preparing to plant rice seedlings in paddy fields in Vietnam.

DID YOU KNOW? Processed maize is used for many non-food items such as glue, paint, dye, fireworks, soap, shoe polish, and aspirin.

Urban Areas

As cities and towns grow and take over natural habitats, many wild animals and plants have adapted to the urban environment. City animals face the dangers of traffic and pollution. Plants grow in parks, gardens, and yards, as well as cracks in walls, in concrete, and on railway tracks.

City Slickers

Birds of prey have moved into urban areas along with leopards, hyenas, and raccoons. Groups of monkeys have also learned to live side by side with humans in busy cities. In 2000, monkeys in Jodhpur, India survived a drought that killed many of their rural cousins.

Urban animals adapt their diet from natural prey to whatever they find. City raccoons have even learned how to open locks and lids.

Nests Everywhere

Animal habits change as wildlife learns to live with the noise of city life, including the movement of traffic. Birds of many kinds have adapted to nest building and raising their chicks in chimney and roof spaces rather than trees.

These white storks have built their nest high above a city in Spain.

Pigeons are a familiar sight in most cities. Many are fed by humans; others are chased away as pests.

Some species of pigeon thrive in urban areas, so they are now found beyond their traditional habitats. Others are on the brink of extinction.

There are more than 300 species of pigeons and doves. They have adapted to nearly all habitats except the hottest deserts and coldest polar regions.

WHEN ANIMALS MOVED TO THE CITY

1. **Baboon:** Cape Town, South Africa, in the 1400s

2. **Hyena:** Harar, Ethiopia, in the 1700s

3. **Brown rat:** London, UK, in the 1720s

4. **Raccoon:** Cincinnati, USA, in the 1920s

5. **Black vulture:** New York, USA, in the 2000s

Brown rats

DID YOU KNOW? Cities offer such good sources of food that some individual birds are no longer migrating.

World Population

In Beijing, there are 6,000 people living per square km—or 14,300 per square mile.

In around 10,000 BCE, when humans began farming, the world population was no more than 10 million—it may even have been as low as 1 million. Since then, the population has grown and grown. There are now 7.6 billion people living on Earth.

Health and Long Life

Human lifespans have radically changed over time. In 19th-century Europe, life expectancy (the age to which the average person lives) was between 30 and 40 years. Today, life expectancy in Western countries is more than 80 years.

In Brazil, favelas are densely packed slum areas that house millions of people in a small amount of space.

Greenland is the twelfth-largest country in the world by area. However, in 2018, it had a population of only 55,877.

WORLD'S MOST POPULATED COUNTRIES

1. **China:** 1.39 billion
2. **India:** 1.33 billion
3. **United States:** 327.63 million
4. **Indonesia:** 265.02 million
5. **Brazil:** 209.45 million

Delhi, India

DID YOU KNOW? Japan has the highest life expectancy in the world, at 83.7 years, followed by Switzerland, at 83.4 years, and then Singapore, at 83.1 years.

The population in Beijing, the capital of China, is more than 21 million, of which 96 percent are Han Chinese.

Population Growth

The World Population Bureau calculates that the world's population growth will reach 9.8 billion by 2050. The growth rate is calculated at about 83 million people per year.

Oman, an Arab state in Southwest Asia, is one of the fastest-growing populations in the world.

Asia

Asia is the world's largest continent. It has the highest and lowest points on the surface of the Earth, and the longest coastline. It has extreme climates, from freezing cold to scorching hot and humid, which support some of the world's most varied animal and plant species.

The caci, a ritual whip fight, is a traditional dance of the Manggarai people in Indonesia.

High and Low

Both the highest and lowest points on land are found in Asia. Mount Everest is in the Himalayas and is 8,848 m (29,029 ft) tall. The Dead Sea, a saltwater lake, is the lowest place on land. It is on the borders of Israel, Palestine, and Jordan, and its shores are 430 m (1,412 ft) below sea level.

Population and Diversity

There are 48 countries in Asia, including the two most-populous countries in the world, India and China, which are home to 1.3 and 1.4 billion people, respectively. In fact, almost 60 percent of all people live in Asia. It contains varied biomes, from treeless deserts to cold coniferous forests and hot and humid rain forests.

Tokyo, the capital of Japan, is the most densely populated city in the world.

ASIA FACTS AND FIGURES

Area: 44.6 million sq km (17 million sq miles)

Population: 4.55 billion (2018)

Number of countries: 48

Largest country: Russia

Smallest country: Maldives

Russia's Volga river

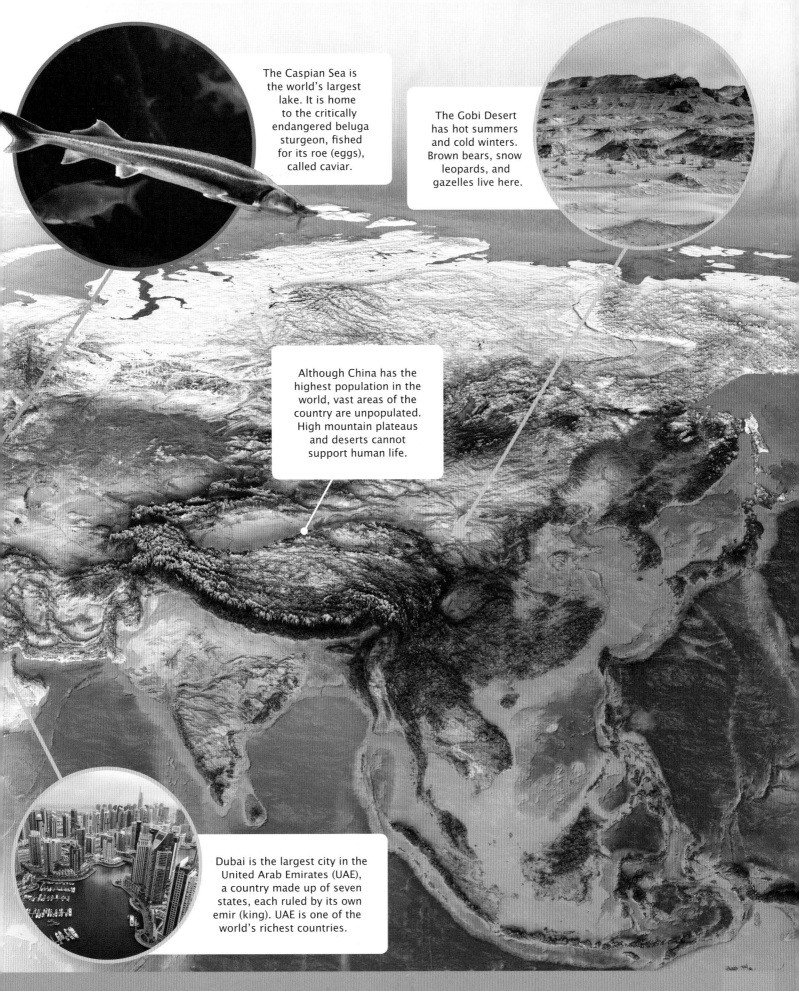

The Caspian Sea is the world's largest lake. It is home to the critically endangered beluga sturgeon, fished for its roe (eggs), called caviar.

The Gobi Desert has hot summers and cold winters. Brown bears, snow leopards, and gazelles live here.

Although China has the highest population in the world, vast areas of the country are unpopulated. High mountain plateaus and deserts cannot support human life.

Dubai is the largest city in the United Arab Emirates (UAE), a country made up of seven states, each ruled by its own emir (king). UAE is one of the world's richest countries.

DID YOU KNOW? Asia has the longest coastline of all the continents, a length of 62,800 km (39,000 miles).

Africa

Africa is the world's second-largest continent. Its biomes include desert, rain forest, mountain forest, grasslands, and wetlands. Mount Kilimanjaro is the highest point in Africa, rising to 5,895 m (19,341 ft). Africa's two most populated cities are Cairo in Egypt and Lagos in Nigeria.

Cradle of Life

Africa is the continent on which human life emerged. We have found fossils of early humans dating to about 300,000 years ago, as well as fossils of our early ancestors, including "Lucy," a female who lived about 3.2 million years ago. "Lucy" had a small skull, like an ape, but walked upright, like a human.

Cities in Africa are growing faster than in any other continent, and by 2034, there will be more than 1.1 billion people of working age in Africa.

Diverse Africa

There are more than 3,000 distinct groups of people in Africa, speaking more than 2,000 languages. Its population is growing rapidly, increasing at a rate of 2.5 percent each year. The Nile, the world's second longest river, stretches for 6,852 km (4,258 miles) from Lake Victoria in Tanzania to Egypt in the north, flowing through nine countries.

The Maasai tribes live in Tanzania and Kenya. They perform the adumu, or "jumping dance," during the coming-of-age ceremony for warriors.

Takamaka, Seychelles

AFRICA FACTS AND FIGURES

Area: 30.37 million sq km (11.73 million sq miles)

Population: 1.29 billion (2018)

Number of countries: 54

Largest country: Algeria

Smallest country: The Gambia, on the continent; offshore, the Seychelles

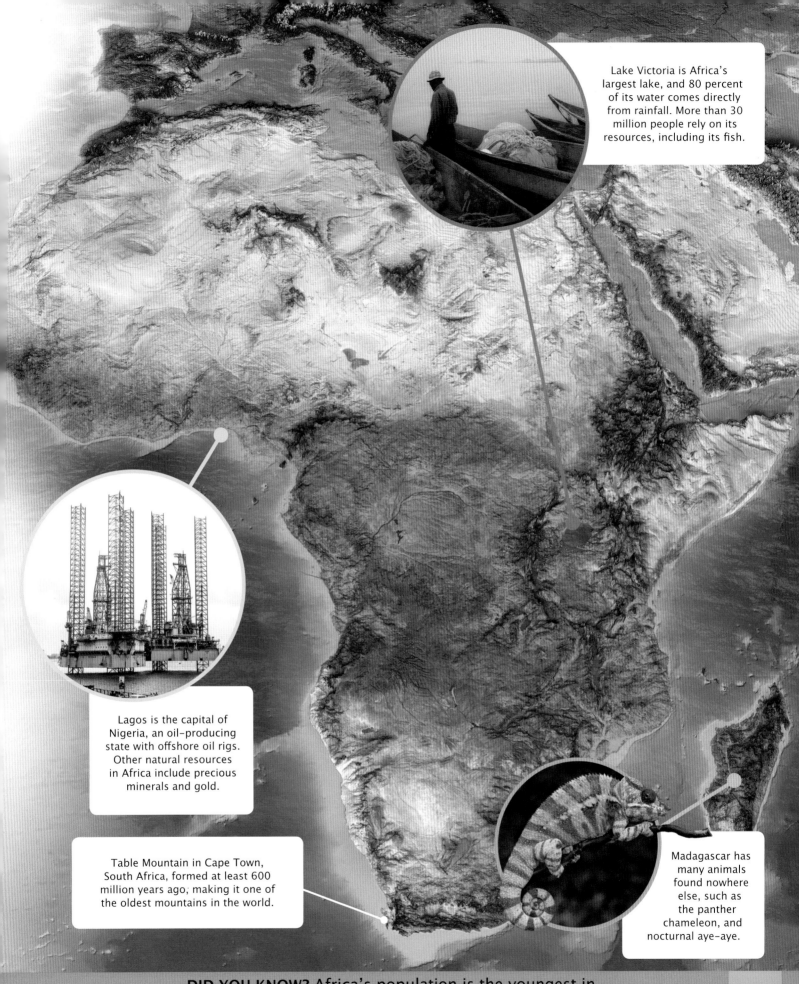

Lake Victoria is Africa's largest lake, and 80 percent of its water comes directly from rainfall. More than 30 million people rely on its resources, including its fish.

Lagos is the capital of Nigeria, an oil-producing state with offshore oil rigs. Other natural resources in Africa include precious minerals and gold.

Madagascar has many animals found nowhere else, such as the panther chameleon, and nocturnal aye-aye.

Table Mountain in Cape Town, South Africa, formed at least 600 million years ago, making it one of the oldest mountains in the world.

DID YOU KNOW? Africa's population is the youngest in the world, with an average age of 19 years 8 months.

North America

North America is made up of Canada, the United States, and Mexico plus Greenland, Bermuda, and the Central American and Caribbean countries. It is the third-largest continent. America is named after the explorer Amerigo Vespucci, who explored the region between 1499 and 1502.

Freezing to Scorching

The climates in North America support a wide range of wildlife. In the far north, Alaska and Canada have boreal forests and snowy tundra covered by permafrost (frozen soil). The scorching Sonoron Desert stretches from California to Sonora in Mexico.

Wolves have adapted to cold habitats. They have thick white fur which blends in with the snow.

North to South

The Rocky Mountains stretch for more than 4,800 km (3,000 miles), from British Columbia in western Canada to New Mexico in the southwestern United States. The north and south are noted for their extremes of weather. The Inuit in the north have icy, windy weather while in Mexico it is hot most of the year.

People in Mexico wear elaborate costumes and face paint to celebrate the Day of the Dead. Up to 3,000 years old, the festival originally celebrated an Aztec goddess, the Lady of the Dead.

NORTH AMERICA FACTS AND FIGURES

Area: 24.7 million sq km (9.54 million sq miles)

Population: 588 million (2018)

Number of countries: 23

Largest country: Canada

Smallest country: Saint Kitts and Nevis

Moraine Lake, Rocky Mountains, Canada

The Inuit live in the far northern regions of Canada, Alaska, and Greenland where living conditions are harsh. They continue to hunt whale, caribou, and seal.

Split Rock Lighthouse on Lake Superior was built in 1910 after the Mataafa Storm of 1905 destroyed 29 ships and took 36 lives.

The original indigenous inhabitants of Cuba were the Guanajatabey people. In 1492, Christopher Columbus arrived on the island and claimed it as a Spanish territory.

Two important ancient civilizations originated in North America—the Aztecs and the Mayas.

DID YOU KNOW? Humans walked to North America from Asia, up to 40,000 years ago, when sea levels fell and the Bering land bridge was formed.

113

South America

The fourth-largest continent, South America has the world's most famous rain forest and river, the Amazon. It also has the Andes Mountains, the Atacama Desert in Chile, and the Pampas Plains.

Language

Brazil, the continent's largest country, was once a colony of Portugal, and is now the largest Portuguese-speaking country in the world. Colonization by Spain also left its mark on South America, and Spanish is an official language of nine countries.

The Nazca Lines in Peru are a series of geoglyphs, lines drawn in the desert rocks. From the air, the lines form geometric shapes and animal figures.

Record Breakers

Five of the world's top 50 largest cities are in South America—São Paulo and Rio in Brazil, Lima in Peru, Bogotá in Columbia, and Santiago, in Chile. The world's longest river is the Amazon, and in the rainy season it is the widest, at 48 km (30 miles). The Amazon rain forest has the greatest variety of plant and animal life in the world.

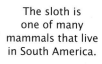

The sloth is one of many mammals that live in South America.

SOUTH AMERICA FACTS AND FIGURES

Area: 17.8 million sq km (6.9 million sq miles)

Population: 429 million (2018)

Number of countries: 12

Largest country: Brazil

Smallest country: Suriname

Brazil's capital city, Brasilia

The Angel Falls in Venezuela is the world's highest uninterrupted waterfall. It is 979 m (3,212 ft) high and is a UNESCO World Heritage site.

The Andes is the longest mountain range on dry land. It is 7,000 km (4,300 miles) long, with a terrain ranging from glaciers to volcanoes, and deserts to forests.

Wearing traditional costume, children pose in the Sacred Valley of the Incas in Peru. The Inca Empire was the largest empire in America before the arrival of Europeans in 1492.

The toucan is one of over 1,300 species of birds that live in the Amazon rain forest—more than 10 percent of the world's bird species.

DID YOU KNOW? The ancient Inca empire covered much of what we today call Peru, Bolivia, Ecuador, Chile, and the northwest part of Argentina.

115

Antarctica

Most of Antarctica is covered by an ice sheet that is up to 4.7 km (2.9 miles) thick. It is the coldest, driest, and windiest continent on Earth. During winter, the sun does not appear above the horizon and the continent stays in complete darkness. There are no trees or shrubs and only two species of flowering plants.

Antarctic Treaty System

Antarctica does not have a permanent human population, only visiting scientists and tourists, so there is no government. Instead it is governed by the Antarctic Treaty System. This prevents military activities and mining in the area and encourages scientific research.

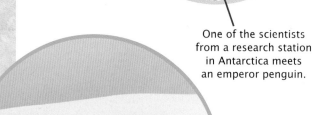

One of the scientists from a research station in Antarctica meets an emperor penguin.

Mountains and Sea

Antarctica is positioned around the South Pole. It is divided into East and West Antarctica by the Transantarctic Mountains between the Ross Sea and the Weddell Sea. The Gamburtsev Mountains stretch for 1,200 km (750 miles) across Antarctica. You might miss them, though, as they are buried under 600 m (2,000 ft) of ice and snow.

In the Southern hemisphere, humpback whales migrate to Antarctica in the summer, when the water is full of krill for them to eat. This whale is breaching.

ANTARCTICA FACTS AND FIGURES

Area: 14 million sq km (5.4 million sq miles)

Population: Depending on the season, between 1,000 and 4,000 people working in research stations.

Temperature: The lowest temperature ever recorded, −89.2°C (−128.6°F), was at Vostock Station.

US Coast Guard ships cut through the sea ice to provide access to McMurdo Station, Antarctica.

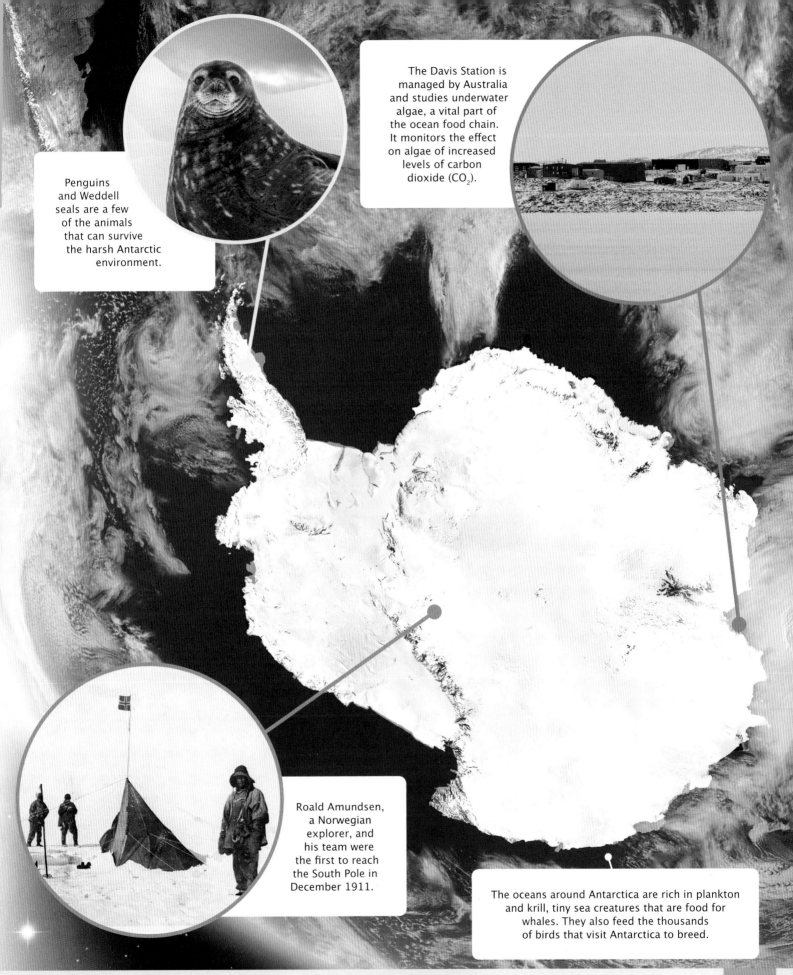

Penguins and Weddell seals are a few of the animals that can survive the harsh Antarctic environment.

The Davis Station is managed by Australia and studies underwater algae, a vital part of the ocean food chain. It monitors the effect on algae of increased levels of carbon dioxide (CO_2).

Roald Amundsen, a Norwegian explorer, and his team were the first to reach the South Pole in December 1911.

The oceans around Antarctica are rich in plankton and krill, tiny sea creatures that are food for whales. They also feed the thousands of birds that visit Antarctica to breed.

DID YOU KNOW? Antarctica is considered the best place to search for meteorites. This is because the cold, dry conditions help to preserve them in good condition.

Europe

Europe is the sixth-largest continent. It was home to two of the world's greatest civilizations, the Roman Empire and ancient Greece. In 1993, the European Union was formed so that countries could help one another with trade, national security, and human rights.

Countries and Borders

The borders of European countries have changed many times over history, as conquering armies advanced and defeated ones retreated. In the twentieth century, two world wars shook the continent, and conflict and political change continue to shape the continent's borders.

Pompeii, near Naples, Italy, is an ancient Roman city that was buried under ash when Mount Vesuvius erupted in AD 79.

European Union

In the late twentieth century, the European Union (EU) was formed. It is now a political union of many countries across the continent that operate as a single market—goods, money, and people can move freely between the countries. It has its own Parliament, flag, central bank, and courts. Sixteen member states use a common currency, the Euro.

In Venice, Italy, there are 118 islands, linked by 409 bridges.

EUROPE FACTS AND FIGURES

Area: 10.2 million sq km (3.9 million sq miles)

Population: 742 million (2018)

Number of countries: 50

Largest country: Russia (straddles Europe and Asia)

Smallest country: Vatican City

Vatican City

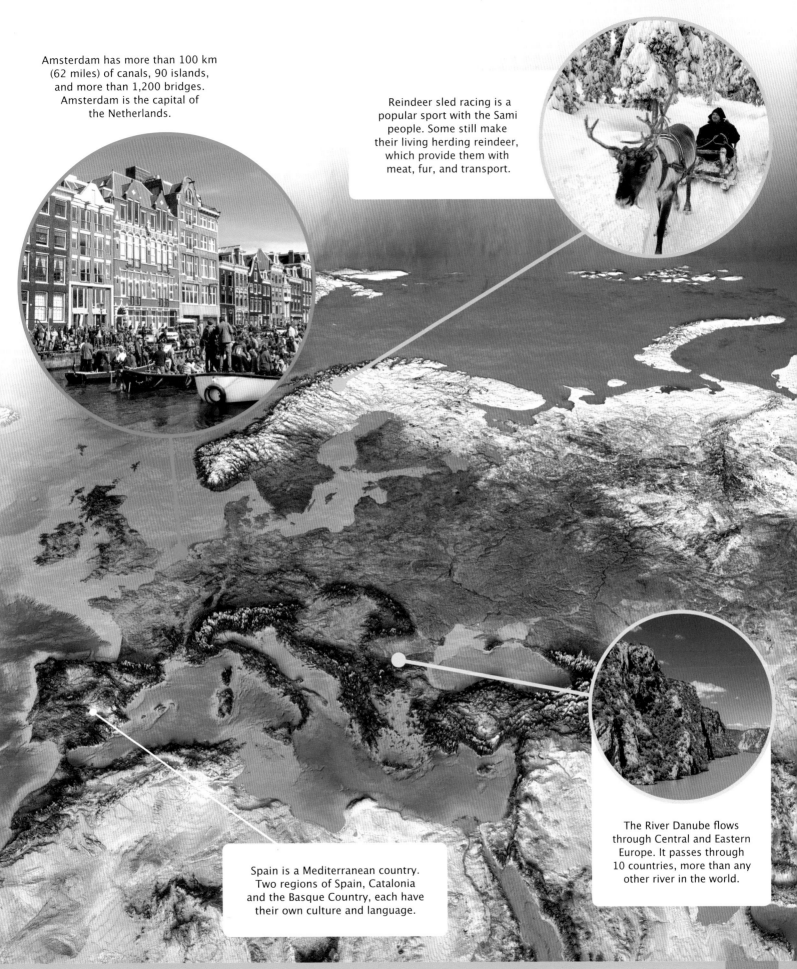

Amsterdam has more than 100 km (62 miles) of canals, 90 islands, and more than 1,200 bridges. Amsterdam is the capital of the Netherlands.

Reindeer sled racing is a popular sport with the Sami people. Some still make their living herding reindeer, which provide them with meat, fur, and transport.

The River Danube flows through Central and Eastern Europe. It passes through 10 countries, more than any other river in the world.

Spain is a Mediterranean country. Two regions of Spain, Catalonia and the Basque Country, each have their own culture and language.

DID YOU KNOW? Denmark has the world's oldest flag. Called the Dannebrog, it was first used in 1307 or even earlier.

Australia and Oceania

Australia is the smallest continent, and the second-smallest in population after Antarctica. Oceania is the region that includes Australia, New Zealand, Papua New Guinea, and the thousands of islands of the South Pacific Ocean.

Islands and Coral Reefs

Oceania includes the Melanesian, Polynesian, and Micronesian groups of islands and coral atolls. In the northeast of Australia is the world's largest system of coral reefs, the Great Barrier Reef. It stretches for over 2,300 km (1,430 miles).

A sea anemone and clownfish on the Great Barrier Reef.

Vast Outback

Most of Australia's interior is sparsely inhabited—a region called the Outback with biomes from grasslands to arid, stony desert. Australia has ten named deserts, and 35 percent of the country is classified as desert. Most of Australia's population live in its big cities, including Perth, Adelaide, Melbourne, Sydney, and Brisbane, along the coast.

The earliest inhabitants of Australia were the Aborigines. This man is making fire.

OCEANIA FACTS AND FIGURES

Area: 8.5 million sq km (3.3 million sq miles)

Population: 40.3 million (2018)

Number of countries: 16

Largest country: Australia

Smallest country: Nauru

Sydney Opera House

Darwin is the capital city of the Northern Territory and is one of Australia's fastest-growing cities.

Fiji is made up of more than 300 islands. Only 100 of these islands are inhabited.

Uluru or Ayers Rock is more than 600 million years old. The sandstone rock is made from compressed sand and was once under an inland sea. It now stands 348 m (1,142 ft) above ground. It takes more than 3 hours to walk around the base of the rock.

The Taupo Volcanic Zone is a volcanic area in North Island, New Zealand, that has been active for the past two million years.

DID YOU KNOW? Highway 1 is the longest network of highways in the world. It stretches for 14,500 km (9,000 miles) around Australia.

Mapping the Earth

Our earliest knowledge of the Earth's lands and oceans has come from brave and adventurous explorers making dangerous journeys to discover new parts of the world. They have been helped by the development of navigational instruments and other technological equipment.

Making Maps

Maps are representations of the land or sea, showing features such as cities, roads, and coastlines. These were originally drawn by hand and not to scale. Today, space satellites and hi-tech graphics software can be used to create accurate and detailed maps in seconds.

Submersibles are usually attached to a platform or larger vehicle at the surface.

Images from satellites in space monitor how our world is changing. This image reveals that forests in Paraguay are being cleared to make fields for farming.

Charting by Stars

The sextant was invented in the 18th century to help sailors navigate around the world. It was used to find the distance north or south of the equator by measuring the distance of the stars above the horizon.

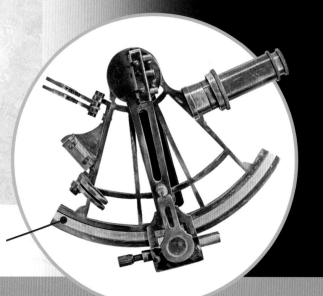

A sextant measures the distance between two visible objects, such as a star or the Moon, and the horizon.

Small submersibles carry experts and equipment to explore and map the deepest parts of the ocean floor and discover what lives there.

Submersibles can explore the ocean's deepest spot, the Challenger Deep in the Mariana Trench, 10,994 m (36,090 ft) down.

MAP TIMELINE

Ptolemy (AD 100–170) wrote a book on how maps could be made by using mathematics and geometry.

Gerardus Mercator developed a world map in 1569, using straight lines to show routes across oceans, which sometimes distorts the size of countries.

The Peters Projection Map, 1973, shows countries in their true proportion to one another.

The Fra Mauro Map, 1450

DID YOU KNOW? The Fra Mauro world map, made in around 1450, has hundreds of drawings and more than 3,000 written descriptions. It took many years to complete.

Looking to the Future

Around the world, childbirth is becoming safer for women. Since 1990, deaths have reduced by 44 percent.

In order to support our growing population, we must find more efficient ways of producing food and homes without damaging the planet. Scientists are constantly working on new ways of reducing our impact on our environment.

Losing Biomes

Huge areas of biomes such as wetlands and forests vanish every year to make way for farming and homes. Yet these biomes are vital to keep out planet healthy. We have to figure out a balance between human needs and protecting our natural resources for the future.

Governments worldwide are trying to control deforestation. But much logging is done illegally and vast areas of forest are difficult to track.

Life on Mars

Space agencies and private companies around the world are figuring out ways humans can live in space or on other planets. NASA wants to send humans to Mars in the 2030s and the private company, SpaceX is also developing technology for a mission to Mars.

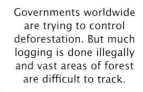

Movies and books are constantly exploring what it would be like to live in space. Could gigantic space ships filled with thousands of humans soon be a reality?

By 2050, 1 in 3 children will be born in Sub–Saharan Africa. Improving child welfare and education, and reducing poverty, are priorities for the future.

Access to health services for all women, including the very poor, means more babies survive.

2011 The international launch of Siri, a voice activated personal assistant app.

2018 The first driverless bus goes into service in Norway.

ARTIFICIAL INTELLIGENCE

The future Robots built to work in hospitals and care homes, looking after the sick and elderly, and designed to do everyday tasks around the house. Robot doctors that use sensors to detect early symptoms of sickness.

Sensing system in driverless cars.

DID YOU KNOW? Terraforming is the process used to make a planet such as the Moon or Mars habitable for humans.

Glossary

ARTIFACTS
A human-made object that has historical or cultural interest.

ATMOSPHERE
The layer of gas surrounding Earth.

ATOLLS
A string or group of islands formed from coral.

BIODIVERSITY
The variety of plant and animal life.

BOREAL
Relating to cold temperate regions in the north where mainly coniferous trees grow.

BRACKEN
A tall fern plant that can cover large areas.

BROADLEAF
Trees that have flat, broad leaves.

BYA
Billions of years ago.

CONIFEROUS
Trees that have cones or needle-like leaves and that are usually evergreen.

CONTAMINATION
Poisoning or making something impure and dangerous.

CRUSTACEANS
An arthropod with a hard shell, such as a shrimp.

DAMS
A barrier built to hold back water forming a reservoir or lake.

DORMANT
Alive but not growing or being active.

ECTOTHERMIC
An animal that heats up its body with warmth from the Sun.

EQUATOR
A pretend line drawn around the Earth that separates it into northern and southern hemispheres.

ESTUARIES
Where water such as rivers flow into the sea.

ETHNIC
A group sharing the same religious and cultural traditions.

EXTINCTION
Becoming wiped out; no longer existing in the wild.

EVACUATED
Moved from a place of danger to a place of safety.

FERTILE
Able to produce more and abundant crops.

FERTILIZERS
Chemicals added to the soil to help crops and plants grow.

FLUORESCENCE
The emission of light from a source that has absorbed light or other electromagnetic radiation, such as an x-ray.

FUNGI
Organisms such as mushrooms and toadstools that reproduce using spores.

GEOMETRICAL
Having regular lines or shapes.

GLACIAL
Icy or ice-like.

GLACIERS
Slow moving masses of ice.

HUMAN RIGHTS
The basic rights of every individual such as freedom from unlawful imprisonment.

HUMIDITY
The amount of evaporated water in the air.

INDUSTRY
Activity such as factories that turn raw materials into things to sell, such as the car industry.

INFRARED
The red invisible light in the electromagnetic light spectrum.

INSULATION
A material that protects something from heat, cold, rain, and so on.

INTERTIDAL
An area of land by the edge of the ocean that is covered with water at high tide and not covered at low tide.

IRRIGATE
To supply with water, as in watering crops.

MICROBES
Tiny microorganisms that can only be seen with a microscope and that my cause disease and sickness.

MIGRATIONS
When people or animals travel long distances from one place to another. Animals do this to go to better feeding or breeding grounds. People migrate when they are seeking a better or safer place to live.

MOLECULES
A group of atoms bound together.

MYA
Millions of years ago.

NATIONAL SECURITY
The safety of a country against threats from another country, such as war and terrorism.

NOCTURNAL
Animals that are active at night, such as bats.

NOMADIC
People that wander around their homeland, usually herding livestock from one feeding ground to another.

OXYGENATE
Supply with oxygen.

PARASITES
Living things that do not produce or find their own food, but instead live on a host that it relies on for food, and gives nothing back in return.

PER CAPITA
Each person in a population.

PESTICIDES
Chemicals or other substances sprayed onto plants and crops to destroy insects and other organisms that do harm.

POLAR AREAS
The regions round the North and South Poles.

POLLUTION
Harmful substances in the air such as fumes from cars, and dust.

PREDATORS
Animals that hunt other animals for food.

PREHISTORIC
The period before recorded history.

RADIOACTIVE
Producing energy in the form of powerful and harmful rays.

RESERVOIRS
Large natural or artificial lakes used as a supply of water for drinking, irrigating land, or helping to supply electricity.

RETRACT
Something, such as claws, that can be drawn back in.

SALAMANDER
Lizard-like amphibian with short legs and a long tail.

SCAVENGE
Search for food or other things through discarded materials and other waste.

SEISMIC
Caused by an earthquake or tremors or vibrations in the earth.

SUBSAHARAN
Geographically, the countries south of the Sahara Desert in the continent of Africa.

SUBTROPICS
Geographic and climate zones located between the tropics and temperate zones north and south of the Equator.

SUCCULENTS
Plants with fleshy stems and leaves that can survive in very dry conditions.

TEMPERATE
From the two regions on Earth between the hot tropics and cold polar regions.

TOXINS
Posionous or dangerous substances created within the body of a living thing can that can harm and kill other living things.

TUNDRA
Flat, treeless plains within the Arctic circle, where the ground is permanently frozen.

ULTRAVIOLET (UV) LIGHT
Light that has the shortest wavelengths and cannot be seen by the human eye.

URBAN
Relating to a town or city.

WEATHERING
When the weather, such as wind or rain, changes the appearance of something by wearing it away.

Index